SHE'S GOT
THE WHOLE WORLD

My Opinion on Love, Life & the Earth as I Feel
See, Believe & Have Grown

I hope it inspires!

GW00320292

SINÉAD McGARRIGLE

Cover Design: Sinéad McGarrigle & Park Lane Communications

Cover Photographs: Michael Sheppard Photography

Book Photographs: Sinéad McGarrigle

Publishers Note: The information in this book is not as a substitute for professional medical advice and treatment. Always consult your health practitioner should you have any health concerns.

First edition printed 2014 in the United Kingdom.

A CIP catalogue record for this book is available from the British Library.

Printed in the UK by GPS Colour Graphics Ltd

ISBN: 978-0-9929288-0-3

Published by Lifetime Health

www.lifetime-health.co.uk

Dedication

My Creator.
To whom I owe my being.

ACKNOWLEDGMENTS

Regarding this book I gratefully acknowledge and wish to thank my best friend and soul mate Brian Devlin who has been more than generous in his understanding, kindness and support whilst I have been completing this book. 'We, like the Swans, are Blessed'. Ray Givans for taking the time to read my book, provide the feedback and write the foreword. Without his help and encouragement it may never have happened. His patience, kindness and generosity are unending, a true gentleman, I am indebted. Of course a special mention also has to go to Eileen his wife, who provided many cups of tea and very nice treats to go with them.

There are also some very special people who have helped me over the years in the good and bad times. Of course deep thanks from my heart to all of my family especially my Parents, I love you both dearly. My 'Warrior' friend Peter Hazzard for his solid friendship and help, Colin Boyd for his absolute faith in me, Sue MacDonald, Caroline McDonagh, Sylvia Williams, Arthur Dodds, Margaret and Brian McKee for their guidance, JJ Brennan for providing a safe haven when I needed it most and Martin Doran for his long standing friendship and unending help throughout the years. Finally, thank you to all of my clients who have each in their special way made a contribution to this book, directly or indirectly.

Credit and attribution to the individual's whose teaching and personal stories have helped many people and also had a positive influence in my life. Buck Buchannan, Richard Moore, Louise Haye, Dr Mike Evans, Ben Stein, Mark Simmerman, Paulo Coelho, Mary Byrne, Archie Barton, Dave from Bromwich, Paul McKenna, Dalai Lama, Eckhart Tolle, Oprah Winfrey, Dr A.T Still, Tony Buzan, Sharon Wright, Jesse Jackson, Nicolas Evans, Bob Dylan, Dr Phil, Albert Einstein, Stephen Covey, Neale Donald Walsch, M Scott Peck, Jack Cranfield, Richard Carlson, B.C Forbes, Dr G Hendricks, Howard Shapiro, Booker T. Washington, Andrew Sercombe, Michael Jordan, William B. Sprague, Theodore Roosevelt, Mark Twain, Napoleon Hill, Jim Rohn, Richard Branson, Martin Luther King, Aldous Huxley, Dr Harry Roberts, Ernest Hemingway, Bradley Whitford, Melodie Beattie, H. Jackson Brown Jnr, Rabbi Harold Kushner, Tsong Tapas, Elizabeth Kubler-Ross, David Kessler, Tim McMahon, Zig Ziglar, Mother Teresa, Winston Churchill, Victor Frankl, Gill Hicks, Nicolas Evans, Maya Angelou, Edward de Bono, Chris Evans, Francois-Marie Arouet and Hilary Rodham Clinton.

CONTENTS

FOREWORD

Sinead's enthusiasm bubbles out from the pages of this book. It cannot help but fill the reader with positivity. The book is well structured, coaxing the reader along, step by gentle step, on a journey where the author has a conversation with the reader, rather than being preachy. Nevertheless, Sinead is scrupulous in drawing examples from her extensive experience as a Life Coach, and from a wealth of reading. The underlying science is carefully weaved throughout the pages, so that the reader is not overwhelmed by technical jargon. She sums this up perfectly at the end, thus:

"The information in this book is not airy fairy, but it is supported by science, you can rewire the patterns in the brain and create new neural pathways all the time."

This book is aimed at those who are prepared to read and take ACTION. It is full of sound advice and humour; full of charity, hope and love. I highly recommend you read this book.

Ray Givans, Author

A MESSAGE FROM SINEAD

Most people treat the present moment as if it were an obstacle that they need to overcome. Since the present moment is Life itself, it is an insane way to live.
Eckhart Tolle

You are now in 'the present moment' of your life. So 'hello', how are you? What brought you to this book store today and why did you pick up this particular book? Are you at a launch of this book or did someone purchase this as a 'gift' to you? Looking for answers? Looking for a bit of direction? Are you a customer of mine, current or previous? Where are you whilst reading this page?

No matter how this book came into your possession, there is a reason why it did. There is a reason why you are still reading. You *are* in the present moment, giving it your attention, just as Eckhart Tolle explains; this is the present moment and life itself. Your life.

This *is* the right thing for you to be doing at this moment in time.

There is absolutely nothing in life that we can be sure of. What we can be sure of is that you were born and you do exist. There are people who exist and then there are those who have a strong desire within them to live and to **live** the **life** they have been given **to the full**. Bob Dylan couldn't have put it better, "Try to be more appreciative, some people just get wet – others feel the rain".

I am throwing down the gauntlet. I am offering you the opportunity to overcome your fears. What greater challenge could I offer?

I WANT TO HELP YOU
FEEL GOOD ABOUT YOURSELF AGAIN.

This is an active book, it requires your participation. If you are genuinely interested in 'feeling the rain' and this is why you are still reading, then great, let's get started. Equally, if it is not, then you can stop reading and walk away from this now.

How To Get The Most From This Book

It is great to be alive and I am delighted that we are going to spend this time together, I'm really looking forward to it. You obviously have a genuine interest in your development and creativity as a human being and are not afraid of thinking *outside* of the box. Alternatively, you are just completely nosy and wanted to see what I would write on the following page! The reason is irrelevant, what is very relevant, is that you made the decision to continue *forward*.

Albert Einstein said 'Great spirits have always encountered violent opposition from mediocre minds. The mediocre mind is incapable of understanding the man who refuses to bow blindly to conventional prejudices and chooses instead to express his opinions courageously and honestly'.

The information in this book is a straightforward expression of my opinions courageously and honestly. It is based on **my life** experiences; my family, friends, work colleagues and equally important, my clients and their life experiences, they are also incredible teachers. I am sure you can think of the many people and incidents in your life that have shaped your opinions, beliefs and so on. I have worked with hundreds of people dealing with very difficult situations express how much their lives have changed for the better through working with me; material I have provided; seminars, workshops, newsletters, advice on books to read and of course the wonderful treatment I provide, Cranio-sacral Therapy. They feel more content in themselves, attitudes have become much more positive, guilt and shame is dissolved and lost its power, family relationships improve, marriages have been re-invigorated, parenting skills have been enhanced, self esteem and confidence has rocketed and personal creativity has flourished. I want you to know that no matter how far you think you've gone down the wrong path, you can *always* turn it around and I will help you also.

I want you to get the best from this book and I also want you to get the very best from me. I want to build a rapport with you the reader and create more of a personal experience. Whilst that can be difficult in a book and to most it will sound crazy, it is possible. All you have to do is be *willing* to read the words, **feel** the meaning express itself <u>for you</u> in your own body and tap into the universal messages intertwined in every molecule of the ink on each page. You *will* engage your deepest being and hear the true voice inside providing the answers as you read. The following suggestions are small and ones you have probably thought of already.

1. Keep an open mind. Take off the blinkers and open your eyes for these are your windows to the world. Come from a position of exploration rather than assuming you know.

2. It can be useful to have a highlighter or pencil handy to mark any areas you wish to read over again or keep as a reference for your own work.

3. Use symbols that mean something to you and help to jog your memory. For example I mark an arrow '→' beside a sentence or phrase of particular interest and importance to me.

4. Keep a journal of notes. To help facilitate this there are blank note pages at the end of each chapter. Reflect over them regularly as it can be helpful to remind and reassure you of how much you have achieved which is usually very motivating and something not very many of us do on a regular enough basis.

5. Stop frequently whilst reading the book to think over what you are reading and ask yourself how and when you can apply it.

6. **Please note**. Confidentiality is essential in my practice and therefore case examples have been altered in name and other particulars to preserve the anonymity of clients without distorting the delivery of the message in the case example being given.

CHAPTER ONE

THE GROUP OPERATIONS DIRECTOR

That's the purpose and aim of all of this. Not to create a belief system that confounds religion, and rejects it. Not to put forth ideas that contradict religion, and replace it. But to reopen the discussion about God in a way that refreshes and reinvigorates our relationship with the Divine.
Neale Donald Walsch

(1) The Group Operations Director & Fear

So here we go, let's begin building that connection together. I thought I would start with the Group Operations Director or G.O.D for short. Whatever your beliefs or response, please try to keep that 'open mind' as requested on the previous page. Even so, I am confident some will still be rolling their eyes right now or have actually put the book down;

'I can't stand any reference to God, at all'
'Oh no, not him, he's caused so much pain'
'Why did he let this happen, why did he let that happen'
'He's not a man he's a woman'

'I'm an atheist so it doesn't matter to me'

'I don't particularly care either way'

What occurred to me when this topic arose was a common thread in the form of what seemed to be 'fear' and I wondered why? And I think it is because nobody really has a 100% certified answer, just an opinion, *their* opinion and interpretation of G.O.D.

The Group Operations Director or G.O.D is a phenomenon. My own thoughts as to why someone may experience or have a 'fear' of G.O.D is because for me, he gives the meaning of 'life'. And what are most people afraid of, **'LIVING'**.

Come on, think about it. So many of us 'exist' but seldom do we follow our dream or dreams, come what may. When was the last time you woke up on a morning and felt great? And I mean, 'felt' really, really great about life, every single thing in your life and your day ahead? When is the last time you felt a soft sun shower on your face and loved it? We hit our crisis in life at twenty, thirty, forty and experience the 'I didn't do this', 'I should have done that'. We reflect on those past years and often feel a failure for not living fully, for being **afraid**. Many of us then blame society, our parents, our peers and anything else we choose to blame for the decisions 'we' have made, some even have the audacity to blame the Group Operations Director!

I ask these two simple questions:

What is *really* to blame, why are you afraid?

_____

_____

_____

When do you want to begin to 'live' and to feel 'alive'?

_____

_____

_____

Is it now or 6 years time? It was Benjamin Franklin who said that many people die at 25 and aren't buried until they're 75. Would you like to wait until you are 70-75 years old and see how you feel about life then? No matter the length of life expectancy, that time is going to go by anyway, so why not do something with it, don't let it die inside you too.

15

(2) G.O.D and his Universal Book

- How many self-help books have you read?
- How many assertiveness courses have you been to?
- How many stress relief articles have you come across in the past few months or year?
- Is this your first time investing in such material?

I think all of us find ourselves at some stage in our lives trying to find ways, any way at all, to help us understand what is going on - relationships, life, freedom, our children and indeed ourselves. You can read M Scott Peck 'The Road Less Travelled', Jack Cranfield 'Chicken Soup for the Soul' or the Dalai Lama to aid your learning but can you imagine sitting in a café reading the Bible? Go with me on this one, there is a point at the end of it.

So conjure now in your mind, you are in the coffee shop, you can see what the coffee shop looks like. You can see what you are wearing. You are sipping a drink of your choice and reading away, engrossed in this book. A friend spies you through the window and pops in to say hello and asks:

'Hey, how are you – I haven't seen you in a while'
'I'm really great thanks, that's a great day isn't it'
'Yes, it's great. So what are you reading?'
'Ah, well actually, it's the Bible'

'!!!!!!'–choking and strange expression on friend's face.

From that second on their opinion of you may well change, sometimes quite dramatically. Generally it can range from 'oh, that's a bit deep' to stamping your forehead with a big stamp that says 'f-r-e-a-k', 'h-o-l-y Joe!'.

And the point is?

On the Bible I wish to suggest only one thing. Is it possible that the Bible *was* the first self help book? Think about it.

(3) G.O.D; Person, Place or Thing?

To describe the Group Operations Director or G.O.D, lets first talk about words and labels. For that is all words are, they are labels that we use to describe a person, place or a thing. Sounds like an English class now but seriously, let us look at some examples.

Example One:

Bessie and Agatha are on a beach holiday and decide to go on one of the local boat trips to see the dolphins. The boat is about to arrive at the dolphins' feeding area and the dolphins are beautiful. Bessie comments 'Look at how they glide through the water, there are a lot of them' and Agatha comments 'Look at how they move, so graceful, I don't actually think there are very many, I thought there would have been more at feeding time'. Both ladies are describing the dolphin's movement in the sea and their *own view* of what *they see*.

Example Two:
Crawford and Sidney are out walking and a beautiful rainbow appears. Crawford comments 'That is glorious' and Sidney replies 'That is superb, and it's a full rainbow, you do not see that often'. Both men are describing the view and their *own view* of what *they see*. Let me repeat the last part of the above sentences. 'Describing the view and **their own view**, of what **they see**. Now repeat it again and replace the words 'their' and 'they' to the singular 'my' and 'I'.

'Describing the view and *my own view* of what *I see'*.

Remember, your eyes are the windows to the world, your world. The words and labels *you choose* allow you to interpret what *you see*, indicating how *you think*, how *you feel* and *your outward physical behaviour* regarding certain situations or issues.

Back to G.O.D, person, place or thing. Forgive me for indulging myself, but I wish to tell this story. I worked in residential homes with the elderly for a number of years and had the good fortune to meet some of the most incredible teachers in my life. There was a lady in particular called

18

Rose who would never participate in the Gentle Exercise Class, she would simply shuffle around the room in what seemed a complete world of her own. She was oblivious to anything going on around her and would mutter nonsensical bits and pieces as she went. This particular day Rose came to the top of the room and stood beside me, I got a chair for her to sit on and she dozed in and out of sleep. More often than not, at the end of the exercise I would help serve the tea and we would maybe sing one or two songs. A resident began to sing a song 'Jesus Loves Me' and some others joined in. At the very end Rose lifted her head from her sleep and in a very stern and clear voice exclaimed to everyone in the room, 'Jesus loves you whether you like it or not'. Needless to say, the residents, nurses and myself were gobsmacked. How profound, what a teacher this woman was.

A world renowned and incredible teacher is the Dalai Lama and this particular piece of advice is powerful.

I believe that at every level of society – familial, tribal, national and international – the key to a happier and more successful world is the growth of compassion. We do not need to become religious, nor do we need to believe in an ideology. All that is necessary is for each of us to develop our good human qualities.
The Dalai Lama

Whether it is a person, place or thing for you or what 'label' you wish to apply; God, Buddha, Spirit, Soul, Life, Religion, the Sea, sitting under your favourite tree reciting a personal Mantra or the Divine. Whatever it is that is driving you and makes you feel 'alive' and 'great' when you awake in the mornings, let it continue to grow and be your own personal guide.

At the end of the day sometimes there is no point trying to make sense of something that just does not make sense to you. Here in chapter one all I am saying is to be comfortable with the level you are at, how you feel, what *you* believe in and as long as it is bringing out the very best in you and your life, keep it very, very close. Also, as the Dalai Lama explained, it is not about becoming religious but developing our 'good' human qualities.

The following is an email I received back in January 2009. The month prior to that was the first time ever the Christmas tree in the White House was to be called a 'Holiday Tree'. 'My Confession' was written by a man called Ben Stein and it was recited by him on CBS Sunday Morning Commentary. Ben's full name is Benjamin Jeremy Stein and he is an American actor, writer and commentator on political and economic issues. He attained his early success as a speechwriter for American presidents Richard Nixon and Gerald Ford and later moved into the entertainment field and became an actor, comedian, and Emmy Award-winning game show host. He has frequently written commentaries on economic, political, and social issues along with financial advice to individual investors and he is also the son of noted economist and writer Herbert Stein who worked at the White House under President Nixon. This is his confession.

My Confession:

"I am a Jew, and every single one of my ancestors was Jewish. And it does not bother me even a little bit when people call those beautiful lit up, bejewelled trees, Christmas trees. I don't feel threatened. I don't feel discriminated against. That's what they are, Christmas trees. It doesn't bother me a bit when people say, 'Merry Christmas' to me. I don't think they are slighting me or getting ready to put me in a ghetto. In fact, I kind of like it. It shows that we are all brothers and sisters celebrating this happy time of year. It doesn't bother me at all that there is a manger scene on display at a key intersection near my beach house in Malibu. If people want a crèche, it's just as fine with me as is the Menorah a few hundred yards away.

I don't like getting pushed around for being a Jew, and I don't think Christians like getting pushed around for being Christians. I think people who believe in God are sick and tired of getting pushed around, period. I have no idea where the concept came from, that America is an explicitly atheist country. I can't find it in the Constitution and I don't like it being shoved down my throat. Or maybe I can put it another way: where did the idea come from that we should worship celebrities and we aren't allowed to worship God as we understand Him? I guess that's a sign that I'm getting old, too. But there are a lot of us who are wondering where these celebrities came from and where the America we knew went to.

In light of the many jokes we send to one another for a laugh, this is a little different: This is not intended to be a joke; it's not funny, it's intended to get you thinking.

Billy Graham's daughter was interviewed on the Early Show and Jane Clayson asked her 'How could God let something like this happen?' (regarding Hurricane Katrina). Anne Graham gave an extremely profound and insightful response. She said, 'I believe God is deeply saddened by this, just as we are, but for years we've been telling God to get out of our schools, to get out of our government and to get out of our lives. And being the gentleman He is, I believe He has calmly backed out. How can we expect God to give us His blessing and His protection if we demand He leave us alone?'.

In light of recent events... terrorist attacks, school shootings, etc. I think it started when Madeleine Murray O'Hare (she was murdered, her body found a few years ago) complained she didn't want prayer in our schools, and we said OK.

Then someone said you better not read the Bible in school. The Bible says thou shalt not kill; thou shalt not steal, and love your neighbour as yourself. And we said OK.

Then Dr. Benjamin Spock said we shouldn't spank our children when they misbehave, because their little personalities would be warped and we might damage their self-esteem (Dr. Spock's son committed suicide). We said an expert should know what he's talking about. And we said okay.

Now we're asking ourselves why our children have no conscience, why they don't know right from wrong, and why it doesn't bother them to kill strangers, their classmates, and themselves. Probably, if we think about it long and hard enough, we can figure it out. I think it has a great deal to do with 'WE REAP WHAT WE SOW.'

Funny how simple it is for people to trash God and then wonder why the world's going to hell. Funny how we believe what the newspapers say, but question what the Bible says. Funny how you can send 'jokes' through e-mail and they spread like wildfire, but when you start sending messages regarding the Lord, people think twice about sharing. Funny how lewd, crude, vulgar and obscene articles pass freely through cyberspace, but public discussion of God is suppressed in the school and workplace. Are you laughing yet?

Funny how when you forward this message, you will not send it to many on your address list because you're not sure what they believe, or what they will think of you for sending it. Funny how we can be more worried about what other people think of us than what God thinks of us.

Pass it on if you think it has merit. If not, then just discard it, no one will know you did. But, if you discard this thought process, don't sit back and complain about what bad shape the world is in".

My Best Regards, Honestly & Respectfully,
Ben Stein

Now write down:

What have I found most beneficial about this chapter:

_____

_____

_____

_____

What do I need to do or in what way could I be thinking better in order to move forward:

_____

_____

_____

_____

Additional Notes:

CHAPTER TWO

TRUE STRENGTH COMES FROM WITHIN

I don't think of myself as a poor deprived ghetto girl who made good. I think of myself as somebody who from an early age knew I was responsible for myself, and I had to make good. It doesn't matter who you are, where you come from. The ability to triumph begins with you. Always.

Oprah Winfrey

When you improve your life, you're physical, mental and spiritual health is healed and restored. Your confidence is restored and your love and respect for *the self* is reinstated. Therefore it only natural, that in this chapter we start with you.

The following exercise is something I use regularly in a workshop setting or with clients on a one to one basis. It is the perfect way to demonstrate **how powerful you are already** by just one, yes, one, single thought. Ensure that you read through this following exercise before you try it and you will need a friend or relative as your guinea pig, so to speak.

1. Have the person stand in front of you and ask them to think of a really negative thought, something that they really do not like, either about themselves or a situation that they did not like at all. They do **not** need tell you what the thought is.

2. Now ask them to raise and extend one arm (left or right, it doesn't matter) out to shoulder level, palm face down. Place your hand on their arm between their wrist and elbow ensuring it is closer to their wrist. Go over point one requesting that they constantly think of that negative thought and really see it in their own mind's eye; what they see, who else is there, colours and so forth, really bring that negative memory in. As they do this, gently push down and their arm will also go down, completely unable to resist.

3. Now repeat the same exercise this time thinking of something great, something fantastic that no-one can take from them, it makes them feel alive and really good inside. It could be someone they love or a favourite outfit, but it really has to make them feel like a million bucks, and again they do not have to tell you what the thought is. Raise the arm to shoulder level and again ask them to constantly think of this wonderful strong thought and to really visualise it; what they see, who else is there, colours and so forth, really bring that positive memory in. As they do this, gently push down and their arm will hardly budge, if at all. **Why is this?**

It is because:

TRUE STRENGTH COMES FROM WITHIN YOU.

Your thoughts create your future, the answers that you look for at any time, are already inside you. If you are constantly creating negative thoughts the answers will more than likely remain questions and you will remain as weak as water unable to cope with the demands of life. If on the other hand, you can create positive thoughts and a positive outlook to life's demands, you will find that your life is not actually as demanding as you had previously thought. You will make more and more positive decisions and feel a sense of 'right, I know what I'm at, I know where I'm going', 'I feel good about this'.

For example, most people have had a period in their life when they did some sort of exercise and exercised quite regularly. If you have you would also know that when you are exercising and giving your body a good workout, you recover quicker and quicker and quicker. Now apply this analogy to dealing with negative thoughts, emotional issues; bereavement or loss of any kind or a relationship that ended when you did not want it to end and other unsatisfactory or untimely events in your life. If you are not exercising your thoughts, emotions and behaviour on the issues that cause you stress and anxiety and getting that much needed 'recovery', you are allowing the building blocks of stress and anxiety to just keep on building. Instead of working out the stress and anxiety and becoming a comfortable human being you keep it all in, get to thirty or forty something and think there is something wrong with you. You become uncomfortable with your life and who you are, why am I here? Why is this happening to me? Why do I feel so bad? In some of the worst cases I have worked with where clients have kept a lid on such high level aggression, sadness, grief, shame and anger, they become completely toxic and so does everything else in their life.

Your mind is an instrument, a tool. It is there to be used for a specific task, and when the task is completed, you lay it down. As it is, I would say about 80 to 90 percent of most people's thinking is not only repetitive and useless, but because of its dysfunctional and often negative nature, much of it is also harmful. Observe your mind and you will find this to be true. It causes a serious leakage of vital energy.
Eckhart Tolle

This is so true. There is no way you will be able to move into a more positive life with a constantly negative mind. It was Socrates who said 'The unexamined self is not worth living' so we are going to examine and explore your 'self' and how healthy your brain is working at present. We are going to move closer to improved physical, mental and spiritual health and a life *worth* living.

Answer the following questions:

1. What are the biggest issues going on in your life at present?

    _____

    _____

    _____

    _____

    _____

2. Have there been stressful times for you in the past few months/years?

    _____

    _____

    _____

    _____

    _____

3. Where do the scars of these stressful times manifest in your body? Do you suffer symptoms for example neck pain or headaches?

    _____

    _____

    _____

    _____

4. What thoughts do you generate in your brain, do they tend to be positive or negative?

_____

_____

_____

5. What effect does that have on the rest of your body?

_____

_____

_____

_____

6. What effect does it have on your behaviour?

_____

_____

_____

_____

Now let us break it down one at a time. First **you're mental well being** and how you are processing your thoughts. For example, when faced with difficulty:

1. Do you respond openly and honestly in situations, especially when they are stressful?
Yes / No

2. Can you walk in the other person's shoes and imagine things from another's point of view?
   Yes / No

3. Is it easy for you to say 'no' to requests from friends or family that you *really do* want to say 'no' to?
   Yes / No

4. When someone says or does something that upsets you; your spouse/partner, best friend or a work colleague, how would you normally respond? Can you handle the issue in a healthy way?
   Yes / No

5. When you are late for an appointment, do you become stressed?
   Yes / No

Is your thought processing/mental well being healthy?
Yes / No

Moving on. Could your mental well being be affecting your physical well being? Let's see.

1. Do you make time for regular <u>structured</u> exercise?
   Yes / No

2. Do you feel properly awake in the morning?
    Yes / No

3. When it gets to 6pm/7pm do you have plenty of energy left over?
    Yes / No

4. Do you have other regular unhealthy physical symptoms; a sore back or neck, headaches, skin difficulties, digestive difficulties, poor concentration, a short fuse?
    Yes / No

> Is your physical well being healthy?
> **Yes / No**

If we bring the two together you will see that your thoughts create your feelings and emotions which in turn will produce your behaviour all of which will positively or negatively affect your nervous system. The cells in your body react to everything; everything you experience and everything you think. If those experiences and thought patterns are negative ones it will bring your immune system down and it will also bring you more negativity. Equally, if you're thought patterns are positive you can boost your immune system and attract more positive experiences. Remember the exercise in chapter two; how strong a positive thought will make you.

The ill effects of thought come about when we forget that thought is a function of our consciousness, an ability that we as human beings have. We are the producers of our own thinking.
Richard Carlson

The main purpose of your brain is for the maintenance of health. It has the extraordinary capacity to receive information, process it and act accordingly. It is the largest organ of secretion in the body producing hundreds of chemicals according to our needs including neuro transmitters used by individual nerve cells to communicate with each other. In this way your brain maintains the balance between your internal physiology; body, thoughts and feelings and your external world, your environment. It is your mind that plays the biggest part and is the biggest factor in the body's ability to heal. As soon as you start to experience physical symptoms it is an immediate indicator from your mind that your body is out of balance. It is at this time you must stop and ask 'What is my body trying to tell me?', 'How am I talking to myself at present?', 'Am I taking good care of myself?'

It is important to exercise your thoughts to help exercise your brain, emotions and physical wellbeing just like Richard Carlson said 'We are the producers of our own thinking'. During the next few chapters I am going to help you decide what the body and mind does need to move toward balance and harmony and help you discover what you love about yourself. We are going to explore what areas of thinking or beliefs you would like to change for the better and how they will benefit your happiness and health now and for the rest of your life. In the meantime:

- Trust that you have the answers
- When a stressful situation arises take time to check-in with your brain; are you providing it with more negatives or more positives?
- Thinking is a useful tool, remember to put it down again every so often.

The following excerpt is in preparation for our next chapter and *you* becoming your own teacher.

And the humble man questioned the Old Man saying, 'I have heard many things concerning your teaching. Yet they say that you proclaim yourself not to be a teacher. What is the meaning of this saying?'
The Old Man stood near, yet he seemed distant and he said, 'I do not teach others, because I cannot teach others, I may only teach myself and everyone teaches their own self all that they learn. We choose that which we desire to know and if you desire to know yourself, you must become your own teacher, and be your own disciple, and learn about yourself'.

The Old Man of the Holy Mountain by Mark Zimmerman

Now write down:

What have I found most beneficial about this chapter:

_____

_____

_____

_____

What do I need to do or in what way could I be thinking better in order to move forward:

_____

_____

_____

_____

Additional Notes:

38

CHAPTER THREE

OPERATING THE MASTER KEY

Think not of yourself as the architect of your career but as the sculptor. Expect to have to do a lot of hard hammering and chiselling and scraping and polishing.
BC Forbes

Anyone who knows me well, will know that I have an innate ability to cut through the woolly bits, the grey areas and there are some clients who have used other terminology to describe this ability also! Rather than hoping to help you find all of the keys that you need to unlock the power within you, we simply get rid of a massive bunch of keys and use just the one.

YOU ARE THE MASTER KEY.

Therein lays the significance of exploring who you are, the genius that you are and fully understanding you *do* have the power within you to do whatever you wish and to feel better about yourself. So what can I do, I hear you ask. We exercise of course, however probably in a different way than what you are used to. I feel this is the first stage of creativity and self development; thinking about actually doing something and taking responsibility for yourself. It is time now, to move away from information simply going in one ear and out the other to physically and internally manifesting new habits. Our aim in this chapter is to fully equip you with the information you need to feel even better about yourself and move toward **positive health** of body *and* mind.

(1) Exercise Nutritionally:

From the moment you were conceived you have been nourished. You are nourished in the womb, as a newborn baby, as a small child and throughout your adult life. It does not change and you need nourishment now and for the rest of your life.

Are you nourishing your body?

You will need to answer this question with 'Yes' or 'No'. If the answer is 'no', I advise these simple steps that may help. Also, you will see written regularly, 'you already have the answers inside you' and this is the same. You know what you should and should not be eating.

✓ **What is healthy and what is not?**
From the following options I would like you to pick a healthy snack. I am holding up in front of you in my left hand a packet

of crisps and bottle of sweetened soft drink and in my right hand a banana and small bottle of water. Pick a hand, which one is the healthy option? Thank you! If you genuinely think crisps and soft drinks are healthier than fruit and natural water try searching for 'healthy eating tips' on the internet or invest in a book that does the same. Regarding other meals, if I offer you deep fried chips, sausage and egg *or* oven cooked poultry with boiled vegetables, potatoes and a glass of milk or water? Which one is the healthy option? I rest my case.

What you eat is critical to the successful running of your body

✓ **Eat foods you like:**
I hope this is self explanatory and this still involves question 1, is it healthy or not? If you think about it, really there is no such thing as 'junk food', only 'food' and 'junk'.

Junk = Junk body

✓ **Three meals per day:**
Breakfast, lunch and dinner. Anything in between should be a snack preferably of fruit or vegetables and should be energising. Paul McKenna writes in his book 'Change Your Life in 7 Days' about a study by Dr Gay Hendricks who invented an easy exercise to determine your very own 'high-energy foods'. After you eat a particular food remain aware of

41

your body sensations 45-60 minutes later. If you feel clear and energetic you ate a high energy food for you, if you don't then you didn't.

✓ **Diets:**

Avoid going 'on a diet'. How on earth do you go 'on' a diet? Stand on top of it, pack a suitcase? Remember our 'words/labels' from chapter one? How about starting your nutritional exercise by just changing the wording from 'going on a diet' to 'I am taking control of what I eat'. Say it again: 'I am taking control of what I eat'. Now, write it down:

_____

2. Exercise Physically:

Tailing on from above, a lot of the time, it may not be the amount of carbohydrates (carbs) you do or do not eat, or the amount of protein we do or do not consume but how inactive we are. Physical exercise is the one that most of us can relate to and maybe know a bit about. So, are you active? Or better still, 'are you active enough? You will need to answer this question with 'Yes' or 'No'. Exercise like food, cannot not be prescribed by amounts because all of us are constructed differently, but again, there are steps that you can take to being active or more active. It is also worth noting that some studies suggest that the positive effects of exercise will last for up to

15 hours after your workout which is pretty incredible. Finally, if you do nothing else out of this book other than take a look at the following video I recommend that you watch, then the outcome has been successful.

Dr Mike Evan's biggest interest is preventative medicine and he wanted to know what the single best thing we could do for our health was. After doing his research he posted a cartooned video on You Tube called '23 ½ hrs'. Like Dr Evan's I love this medicine for the breadth of conditions it can benefit and how easily it can be implemented to *really work* for so many different health concerns. I am only going to give you a few examples from his research. However I highly recommend you watch the full video. When this treatment was applied:

- **Knee arthritis** was reduced by 47% in patient's pain and disability with a prescription of one hour, three times per week.

- **Dementia and Alzheimer's** progression in older patients was reduced by 50%.

- Patients with **high risk of Diabetes** coupled with other lifestyle intervention reduced progression to Frank Diabetes by 58%.

- It is the number one treatment for **fatigue.**

- With a prescription of 4 hours per week for **post-menopausal** women gave a 41% reduction in the risk of hip fractures.

- In a large-scale meta-analysis confirmed a whopping 48% reduction in **anxiety**.

- Patients suffering from **depression** reduced to 30% on a low dosage which increased to a 47% reduction when the dose was increased.

- Following over 10,000 Harvard Alumni over 12 years those that had this treatment had a 23% chance lower risk of death than those who did not receive the treatment.

Of course the main outcome from this treatment is quality of life and **making your life better**. So what is the treatment?

WALKING.

Notice 'walking', not triathlons. You will have to log on to YouTube to find out what the '23½ hours' is though. If you do not have a computer I am sure the local library or a friend/relative will be more than happy to help. So….

- ✓ Ensure that the activity you are involved in coincides with happiness. If it doesn't make you happy don't do it, find something that makes you happy when doing it.

✓ Think about the exercise you are currently doing. A lot of people are not even aware that they are already physically active. Gardening, walking the dog and housework are all physical activities and if you have kids they will certainly keep you active!

✓ Take it up a notch. If you are doing the housework put on your favourite music and get your hips moving with that hoover. When walking the dog make the step that little more brisk. When taking the kids to the park get those arms working by pushing the swing, better still get on the swing next to them.

✓ Sex. On average sex burns 150 to 250 calories per half hour and it is widely documented that sex is good exercise. Howard Shapiro MD, a New York City weight-loss specialist and author of books including *Picture Perfect Prescription*, puts it this way: "If someone has a healthy sex life, they will be less frustrated and people eat less when they are not frustrated". Also endorphins are the brain's feel-good chemicals and because sex is a mood enhancer; the more you have it, the more endorphins are released.

3. Exercise Your Brain:
As talked about in chapter two your brain makes countless adjustments, secretions and commands which it sends out to

the rest of your body, which is why you may wish to start thinking about giving it a bit of loving. You possess one of the most valuable and powerful pieces of equipment in the world, right between your ears. Some of the following may help.

✓ Try a crossword puzzle, jigsaws or purchase a board game. It can also be useful to read a book on the power of the brain, for example, 'Mind Mapping' by Tony Buzan.

✓ 'Shift your brain space' is a term I have used for many years. After my own personal traumas I became very aware of my warning signs and strong negative voices in my head was one of them. I would say to my partner 'I just need to go away and shift my brain space'. What I meant was that I needed to do something to bring my brain back into harmony. I would literally take a few minutes, be still and ask myself, what do you need? It could be anything; go for a walk, have a coffee and just *sit down*, listen to music or sing along. When it was not possible to go for a walk, I would think the most beautiful thoughts that I could; of someone I love, my favourite holiday or dream that I want to become reality.

✓ Be the loving operator of your own mind and say this out loud. 'I am the loving operator of my brain'.

✓ Treat it like the most beautiful garden, with stunning waterfalls, beautiful orchids and regularly clear out the weeds, visualising actually weeding out the garden of your mind.

Also, because our brain *is* so powerful, precious and works incredibly hard for us, it is also equally important to rest it. Sometimes, we just think too much! If you find that the head is too busy with 'mental chatter' you may wish to invest in other products that I provide such as the Self Development Motivational CD and Mindfulness Relaxation CD. In both I teach proven powerful mind programming techniques that you can use at home to relax the mind, help reduce stress levels, release tension in your body and feel even happier in yourself.

The brain is God's drug store having within, all drugs, lubrication oils, opiates, acids and every quality of drug the wisdom of God thought necessary for human happiness and health. The motility expressed by the brain is thought to have an important influence on the way these chemicals are produced and distributed.
Dr A.T Still, Author & Teacher of Craniosacral Therapy

4. Exercise Your Foundations:
Let's take an example here – 'you'. As you are sitting there now, think of your age. Reflect back over the video of your

life; every fall as a child, every wrong decision you have made, any bones you may have broken, every ice cream that dropped to the ground, every relationship you ended, every relationship that ended when you did not want it to, any time a parent shouted at you, any time you shouted at someone younger than you or any other traumatic experiences – all stored in your body. They are your foundations that have been gathering information like candyfloss on a stick or snow on a snowball until it is so big, we can't cope and feel the snowball is too big to melt and the candyfloss is now too sickening to eat in that irritable stomach.

- What are your foundations built on? What are the main negative/positive life experiences that have affected you?

_____

_____

_____

_____

- How solid are your foundations?

_____

_____

_____

- Which ones are healthy and which ones are not?

  _____

  _____

  _____

- Which ones can you deal with yourself and which do you need help with?

  _____

  _____

  _____

- Who do you need to thank or who do you need to forgive?

  _____

  _____

  _____

- Who do you need to go and talk to; a parent, brother/sister, your friend or a professional such as a GP, counsellor or careers advisor.

  _____

  _____

  _____

When looking at our foundations it can be complex especially if throughout our lives there has been great difficulty. It is important to remember that whilst our blue print, our foundations have helped shape us, they do not define who you are now or who you can become in the future, please remember that.

Success is not to be measured by the position someone has reached in life, but the obstacles he has overcome while trying to succeed.
Booker T. Washington

5. Exercise Your Choices:

We are not animals. We are not a product of what has happened to us in our past. We have the power of choice.
Stephen Covey

This is a brief introduction to 'choice' and something we will continue to look at throughout this book. You have previously learnt from your parents, peers, other children, teachers and even your pets, all of which have influenced the choices you have made so far in life. But now as an adult you are in charge, you are learning from you!

YOU OWN YOU'RE LEARNING & YOU OWN YOUR CHOICES.

If you own it and you learnt it, you can also unlearn it and replace it with something that suits you better and *feels* better. You have a choice and no-one, not even the Group Operations Director (G.O.D) can make your choices for you. You are responsible for *all* of your thoughts and have a choice how you think. You are responsible for *all* of your feelings and have a choice how you wish to feel. You are responsible for *all* of your behaviour and have a choice how you behave. You are responsible for *all* aspects of your health and physical well-being and can choose whether or not you will exercise the outer body, bones, ligaments and muscles.

What I am saying, is that in order to successfully operate the Master Key which is YOU – *YOU* need to go and sort it out! It is as easy as flicking through the channels on TV. You have the power of 'choice' to change the channel of your life at any stage. If you do not like the channel you are on, change it by making the choice to do so. If you are reading this now and have stuck it out, then great, because you are obviously at 'amber'. Only you can hit the 'green' light to go. Take your foot off the break and hit the accelerator - YOU CAN melt that snowball if you choose to and remember:

Taking **Responsibility** = Knowing You have a **Choice**= Control of your **Destiny**

Do you want to be the master of your fate or the victim of your circumstances?

If you find that your 'Master Key' is not turning in the lock as effectively as you would like always double check how you are thinking and talking to yourself. For example when you ask yourself the question "Why can't I do this" your mind will immediately start to search for all of the reasons why you can't do it – the negatives. If you simply re-word the question to "How can I most easily make this work" or "What would be the most beautiful way I can handle this" your mind will immediately start to search for all of the ways in which to make it work – the positives. Practice phrasing it in your own positive way. Other examples include:

- What is the most productive way I can solve this problem?
- How many different ways of solving this problem can I come up with?
- How can I most easily **stop** _____.
- How can I most easily **start** _____.

It is these types of questions that will create a more resourceful position for you, The Master Key to operate from, so keep practicing.

I've missed more than 9000 shots in my career. I've lost almost 300 games. 26 times I've been trusted to take the game winning shot and missed. I've failed over and over and over again in my life. And that is why I succeed.
Michael Jordan

Now write down:

What have I found most beneficial about this chapter:

_____

_____

_____

_____

What do I need to do or in what way could I be thinking better in order to move forward:

_____

_____

_____

_____

Additional Notes:

CHAPTER FOUR

TAKE ACTION

Do not wait to strike till the iron is hot; but make it hot by striking.
William B. Sprague

Everything in your life so far has been learnt by you from the people you spend time with, your environment how you look after yourself and so on. It was Alvin Toffler an American writer and futurist who said 'The illiterate of the twenty-first century will not be those who cannot read and write, but those who cannot learn, unlearn, and relearn'. So what about you? Are you going to be literate or illiterate about your future?

If your life at the minute is completely fantastic then that is great, you don't have to do anything and you must be reading this book out of interest. However, if your life is not how you want it to be, don't panic either! Sit down and write out what those things are and then brain storm the ideas beside each one again utilising the tips in chapter three 'Operating the Master Key'. But, you must remember that for any of this to work it is going to be impossible to do without change. Should that be a thought process or a deeply held belief about a situation or person, whatever it is, nothing in your life is going to change if *you* cannot change. If you have big decisions to make take action now, otherwise you just add to the baggage and carry it on into the next day, the next week or next year of your life.

Our lives occur in transitions. For instance, people aged 40-45 years old are centred on the growing awareness of one's own mortality and the realisation that the dreams of one's youth may never be realised. If you are reading this book and are nowhere near that age, there is no harm in just thinking about it now. When you do look back on your youth and your life:

- What is it that you want to see?
- Who is the person you want to be?
- How would you like to be thought of by others?

Let's take stock.

- What changes/decisions are you thinking about now?

_____

_____

_____

_____

_____

- What is it, small or big that **you** could do to get you a little closer to feeling better about life and about yourself?

_____

_____

_____

_____

_____

Twenty years from now you will be more disappointed by the things that you didn't do than by the ones you did do. So throw off the bowlines. Sail away from the safe harbour. Catch the trade winds in your sails. Explore. Dream. Discover.
Mark Twain

You are in a fantastic position to take action because you have a choice, **we all do**. The following are universal aspects in life that people sometimes become or are, unhappy with:

Home Life:

This can vary immensely; financial strain, becoming new parents, sexual/intimacy issues, substance or alcohol abuse, children with anti-social behaviour issues, physical/mental abuse or general unhappiness in the home. Sometimes it can be something as simple as setting time aside, even half an hour to spend with your wife/partner, kids, parent(s) either playing or chatting about the issue causing the unhappiness or just how you are all getting on at present in that relationship as a couple, family and so on. Where cases are more severe it is incredibly important to seek help, there are a multitude of organisations that you will find either from local newspapers or via the internet. If your home life is really good this could be just a reminder to keep the communication going and reinforcing the need to get time together.

Health Concerns:
This can vary from acute neck or back pain that is debilitating, to terminal illness. It is important to explore how you are thinking about the health issue or concern and also to consider if it would be helpful to speak with a professional. This can help with any emotions surrounding the issue; loss, power, guilt, time, fear, anger, patience, surrender, forgiveness, acceptance and happiness.

Occupational Life:
If you are unhappy in your current work environment or would like a change, write down the things you like and dislike about the job. Weigh up the pros and cons, speak with family and friends and also seek out a career's advisor to aid the process.

Social Life:
What hobby you would like to re-ignite or begin to get

involved with? What friends have you not seen in a while that you would like to catch up with? What things did you previously do that you don't do anymore? For example go for walks, visit a favourite coffee shop and read a book or a social night out.

The Soul Mate in Your Life:
This could be airing your feelings regarding something or wanting to organise something you would really like to do together like dancing lessons! Make it happen.

In any situation, the best thing you can do is the right thing; the next best thing you can do is the wrong thing; the worst thing you can do is nothing.
Theodore Roosevelt

That is why this chapter is called 'Take Action'. As much as 'thinking' positively is important it is pointless if it is not positively 'actioned'. I cannot say for fact that *nothing* will ever happen without action, there is a lot to be said about the divine universe and things unfolding naturally and beautifully. What I am explaining is that if there is something specific you wish to do or a goal you wish to achieve you will need to organise and put a structure in place to achieve it. For example if I want to kick a rugby ball between the posts, that is my goal. Before I move toward the ball I mentally must have the desire for it to go between the posts and also a strong belief that it will and finally the act of kicking the ball is the action.

Goal:

First decide what it is that you want to achieve and have a very clear image of it down to the detail of how it will unfold.

Intention & Desire:

The law of attraction states that what you focus on you will get. Therefore you must actively bring focus and attention to what it is you wish to achieve.

Belief:

People become remarkable when they start to believe in themselves and what they wish to achieve. Thinking is not enough. You must visualise and generate in your body what it will **feel** like for you when you achieve your goal. Continue to visualise in order to keep experiencing those feelings attracting it even more.

Action:

Success is connected with action. Successful people will keep on moving, yes they'll make mistakes but they won't quit. Also, your life is 10% what happens to you and 90% how you react to it. You may well come up against hurdles, some you were expecting and some you were not. Make the choice to stick with it, it will be worth it in the end. Stopping is like slashing your other three tyres because you got one flat one. Keep on going, chances are you will stumble on something wonderful perhaps when you were least expecting it. You'll be hard pushed to stumble on anything sitting down!

Structure:

I cannot stress enough the importance of structure. Most things we do have a structure and it is important that you have structure in anything you wish to achieve. Take something as simple as making a cup of tea.

1. Turn on tap for water
2. Fill kettle with water
3. Place kettle on holder and switch on to heat water
4. Get additional items required; favourite cup, milk, sugar, teabag
5. Place teabag in cup and add hot water, milk, sugar as required
6. Enjoy

If you are unsure of how to make a start the following is a simple way of structuring goals and can be useful to help clarify and prioritise goals if you have more than one. If you look at our cup of tea goal you will see six stages to our structure that takes the task from conception to completion.

61

You may have three stages or ten to complete a goal, adapt in whichever way you find most beneficial to you. The following details the actual information I had on my plan in order to complete this book. Use your imagination and create a layout that suits with a personalised title for you; 'My Personal Excellence Plan' or 'This Month's Goal Chart'. Regarding time frame again, you need to personalise. Whilst the example given is varied over several months I was doing at least one thing, big or small every single day of the week to meet the 4 goal points, I felt I needed that type of daily discipline. You may need something daily, weekly or fortnightly.

Goal: Get a handle on completing my book.		
	Action to be taken:	**Date to be completed:**
1	Establish what I currently have re: chapters/titles and get it fresh in my head.	29 Aug 2011
2	Diary and translate outstanding tapes and notes.	22 Oct 2011
3	Complete outstanding chapters.	30 Nov 2011
4	Research how the book will be published: editor/printing/costs/download?	15 Dec 2011
5		

Decide what action you feel is best to take and in what order to reach your goal. I always sleep on it to reflect and make any final adjustments the next day. Remember this is a guide and I have not always got the desired outcome I hoped for, but as mentioned earlier keep moving, make the mistakes and move on.

Additional advice I wish to give you regarding change and taking action is based on two small words 'yes' and 'no'. These are two of the smallest words in the dictionary that can have a huge negative or positive impact on life and unfortunately I did not use the latter of the two as much as I should. What would happen is that I would say 'yes' to pretty much everything; helping someone out, change of times to go out, going out when I didn't want to and so on. The outcome was that I got nothing done myself and found that I had become all things to all people. You simply cannot sustain that and of course neither could I, it was exhausting. I did not acquire the ability to say 'no', and actually feel comfortable with it, until my mid-thirties. We as human beings generally struggle with saying 'no'.

- "NO, it would be too much of a rush for me, can we make it 7.30pm instead of 7.00pm?"
- "No, I don't want to go out tonight, I am really looking forward to a night in; hot soak in the bath, jammies and a DVD."

Practice making the right decisions for you and practice saying 'no' when you really need to always checking:

- Am I making mature decisions?
- Deep down are they the right choices for me?
- Am I taking action?
- If I continue this way where will I end up?
- Is this what I want for me?

Allow the body and mind to be open to new input to help cultivate your decisions but most importantly, activate within you:

ACTION
ACTION
ACTION

No matter what your goal, ensure *that* is what you think about. Remember what you think, you attract. If it financial strains at home do not constantly talk about what you cannot afford or that you are constantly overdrawn otherwise that is exactly what you will get more of. Focus on prosperity not debt, focus on feeling completely healthy and in harmony not illness and disease, focus and visualise yourself in a loving relationship not on all past negative relationships, focus on the job of your dreams and so on. Finally, let go. I had no idea how I was going to finish this book or how on earth it was going to be published. I utilised all of the techniques detailed in this book and the next thing I know, I'm finalising the cover of the book and it is going to print. Trust and let go.

We are the inventors of our lives; we are the ones setting sail on this voyage of discovery. The world is not open to just some people, it is open to everyone and that includes you. The following is a fantastic short story teaching us much about the possibilities if we take a step back and see if there is another path that may be better for us.

How The Path Was Forged

One day a calf needed to cross a virgin forest in order to return to its pasture. Being an irrational animal it forged out a tortuous path full of bends, up and down hills.

The next day a dog came by and used the same path to cross the forest. Next it was a sheep's turn, the head of a flock which upon finding the opening led its companions through it.

Later, men began using the path: they entered and left, turned to the right, to the left, bent down, deviating obstacles, complaining and cursing and quite rightly so. But they did nothing to create a different alternative.

After so much use, in the end, the path became a trail along which poor animals toiled under heavy loads, being forced to go three hours to cover a distance which would normally take thirty minutes, had no one chosen to follow the route opened up by the calf.

Many years passed and the trail became the main road of a village, and later the main avenue of a town. Everyone complained about the traffic, because the route it took was the worst possible one.

Meanwhile, the old and wise forest laughed, at seeing how men tend to blindly follow the way already open, without ever asking whether it really is the best choice.

Paulo Coelho

Now write down:

What have I found most beneficial about this chapter:

_____

_____

_____

_____

What do I need to do or in what way could I be thinking better in order to move forward:

_____

_____

_____

_____

Additional Notes:

CHAPTER FIVE

LOVE & LOVING RELATIONSHIPS

Love is an untamed force.
When we try to control it, it destroys us.
When we try to imprison it, it enslaves us.
When we try to understand it, it leaves us lost and confused.
Paulo Coelho

This chapter is two-fold 'love' and 'loving relationships' and first we will talk about 'love' and the act of 'loving'.

Our human condition can allow us to perform great deeds and to love greatly but unfortunately the opposite is also true. We so easily write people off–we write 'human beings' off, simply because they are out on the street or the face just does not fit. I would urge you to be more humane and treat people with respect, regardless of what they do or do not have – you never know how far reaching your love in the form of basic 'kindness' could be for them.

The word 'stagnant' means not circulating or flowing, not growing or changing and that is what our love towards strangers has become.

STAGNANT; WITHOUT FORCE OR VITALITY.

I am not talking about donating all of your life savings to someone on the street or giving away your house, but the basic charity that begins in your home, within our own communities and also when we travel. Seeing someone in need and just offering a kind thought or gesture such as a smile can change the energy in a room and can bring about 'change' full stop.

I want you to make it your business to watch a short story that was written, directed and produced by Sharon Wright. Key into any search engine 'Change for a Dollar' and watch the video from start to finish. If you get stuck I am certain a friend or relative will help you, or go to your local library and use the computers there. If at all possible stop now and watch the short story before you continue reading. Sharon has nailed the very essence of the effect *we all* have on others and the change you can make without even realising it. Thankfully there are fantastic testaments of love throughout the world and I particularly like the one I am going to share with you now about the Dalai Lama's 'hero'. This story is not just about love but forgiveness which we will look at closer in chapter eight.

In 1992 Richard Moore walked the Choctaw Trail of Tears across the State of Mississippi, a 240 mile trek in 2 weeks, and then decided to set up his own charity in 1996 called 'Children In Crossfire'. Based in Derry in Northern

Ireland, the charity runs projects in Africa, Asia and South America focusing on issues that affect children; provision and access to clean water, food, health and education.

Years later on the 17 July 2007 His Holiness the Dalai Lama was key note speaker at the Children In Crossfire's 10th Anniversary conference in Derry, when he told Richard "Whether you believe it or not, you are my hero, and a wonderful son of humanity. Despite your tremendous painful experience you don't have any anger or hate. You accept what has happened and keep your peace of mind. You are a good example and model."

Why did His Holiness the Dalai Lama say this? Was it because Richard had achieved the amazing feat of walking the Choctaw Trail of Tears or because he set up a much needed charity for children? No. It was because at just 10 years old Richard was shot and blinded by a rubber bullet fired by a British Soldier in 1972 on his way home from school and has since met and befriended the same soldier in 2006.

During his visit the Dalai Lama met privately with Richard and Charles (the soldier) and said that he hoped Richard's story would be told to everyone as a source of hope, which is one of the reasons I decided to include it in this book. The Dalai Lama went on to say "It is wonderful to see the person who suffered and the person who caused the suffering become true friends, there is genuine friendship and happiness which is based on forgiveness."

In 2011 the Dalai Lama gave three talks in Dublin, Kildare and Limerick where he delivered some beautiful and simple messages that we can all benefit from. Asked when he last had laughed he said that he did so from morning to night, and began again the next day. On the subject of anger and hatred he told an audience 'It has no effect on your enemy, only on you. Use intelligence instead to bring some benefit to you and the perpetrator'. The celebrated promoter of non-violent means to solve conflict said that the 21st century must be about dialogue because millions of people have been killed and limitless others have suffered. Yet armed struggles continue, 'compassion' he insisted is a simple virtue to practice.

So, what did you think love was for? The times when you feel 'in love'. The times when you are 'loving' because someone is being loving to you. Of course not. Love is not just for the loving times but also the really tough times *and* the people you find it tough to love.

I said at the start of this chapter, we do, we so easily write other human beings off and constantly judge but it is so important to practice compassion to others who may have been less fortunate than ourselves.

"We ride rough shed over the feeling of others, getting our own way, finding fault, issuing threats, criticise a child or an employee in front of others without even considering the hurt to the other person's pride. Whereas a few minutes of thought, a

considerate word or two, a genuine understanding of the other
person's attitude would go so far to alleviating the sting! In
other words, do onto others as you would have them do unto
you.

Dale Carnegie

Love is kind and I think if we could look into people's hearts and minds and see the challenges they are facing we would be a bit more kind and considerate more quickly. Are you prepared to grow toward the people you may need to love a bit more with patience, kindness, care and compassion? Eventually you will have to take responsibility for what you see in people and be honest about how you love different types of people.

Loving Relationships.

When two people are following their goals they may work at different speeds and the goals may be different. Thus unsettling emotions can sometimes arise. A common situation is when the quality of love being given is not reciprocated it can often result in feeling 'I am taking all the responsibility for making this relationship work with very little in return'. This equals a feeling of being undervalued with little in the form of thanks or appreciation for your efforts, and your good nature is being taken for granted. Then you meet someone new, of the same sex or not, who just seems like a breath of fresh air and you find yourself questioning your current relationship and also yourself. Scrap yards are a good analogy for describing relationships. I know - you may be thinking, where exactly are you going with this one Sinéad? But bear with me.

A guy I know was telling me this story about how he wanted some parts for his car and to save money he was going to get them at a scrap yard rather than from the manufacturer. The first yard he went to was a complete mess and he struggled to find the particular make of car he needed never mind the wing mirror and the staff in the yard didn't seem to have a clue either. He left slightly irate at his experience. The second yard on the other hand, was a complete surprise. The whole yard was sectioned out according to the car manufacturer which made it easy to access his make and model of car and the part he was looking for. An added bonus was that the staff knew their business thoroughly. My friend decided it was an extremely well run business, respected the owner and decided to make his purchase there.

Relationships are a little bit like a scrap yard. Decent enough cars, vans and so on that have had their little dents and scrapes and others with some serious knocks. Here's my point. The scrap yard can be likened to the guy or girl and the little scrapes they have had, or complete crash and burn experiences that may have resulted from previous relationships or life experiences in general. If you are feeling unsettled about who you are with, questions need to be asked.

- How do they store their parts; body, mind and emotions?

- We all have scrap/baggage. Is their baggage processed in a healthy manner or messy and negative? For example, can they talk about their difficulties or do you feel they take it out on you? Or do they resort to something else to deal with it; drugs, alcohol.

- Is the person you are currently in a relationship with a complete mess?

- Does their scrap yard have a **negative effect on you** or a **positive effect on you**?

- Do you want to get out of that yard and visit the new showroom or do you feel it will be worth it to stay and try to help this person tidy up their scrap yard?

On the other hand is the guy or girl a complete surprise? They know exactly who they are and what they are at. They know their business thoroughly and inspire you. Whilst yes, they have had their little run-ins and possibly some crash and burns with what life has thrown at them but, they have addressed it and made some positive decisions on how to handle it. They are emotionally stable, allowing **you both** to have a healthy and understanding relationship. If your 'other half' does the things that turn you on; brings happiness into your life, listens, is efficient, makes you even more productive and is genuinely good for you, the likelihood is that you will respect, love and cherish them for it *and* for a very long time. When you both do come up against difficult times, you can work through it together and support one another.

If on the other hand they do nothing to move themselves or the relationship forward, you will generally tend to worry, anxiety kicks in and you will eventually disrespect them to the point where you cannot stand the sound of them breathing. What is even more detrimental is the effect on you in the form of low self esteem, a loss of usual confidence and general lack of self-worth, which can be incredibly damaging. Think of a relationship you are in at present, it can be intimate or not, loving or not. Try this exercise:

Do they bring out the best in me?
Yes / No / Sometimes

Do they make me more productive or less productive?
More productive/ Less productive / There is no change

Do they give me more energy or drain me?
More energy / It can be draining / I'm drained

Am I *even* happier and more fulfilled?
Yes / No / Sort of

Are they understanding?
Yes / No / Sometimes

Do they listen to my needs?
Yes / No / Sometimes

Are they kind?
Yes / No / Sometimes

Is this a truly loving relationship that I am happy to be a part of?
Yes / No / Sometimes

Is this person good for me?
Yes / No

You can use the above questions if you are ever unsure about a relationship and as long as you answer them honestly it will reveal quite clearly whether it is a healthy relationship for you or not. If someone wants to be a part of your life they will make the effort to be in it, in a positive and beautiful way, no excuses. If you are in a relationship or friendship that is making you painfully unhappy then it may well be time for you to make a change. Sometimes we stay in a relationship simply because they feel safe and familiar even when they are bad for our personal growth and creativity. A true partnership provides a safe place that encourages *mutual* growth and creativity.

You'll find another love who does want to put in the effort required and to be honest, if its right, it should not feel like an effort. At the end of the day you will meet new friends and new loves but you are not going to find another you. I would like to finish this chapter with a psalm I read many years ago at my best school friend's wedding:

__Love__ is patient, __love__ is kind.
It does not envy, it does not boast, it is not proud.
It is not rude, it is not self-seeking, it is not easily angered, it keeps no record of wrongs.
__Love__ does not delight in evil but rejoices with the truth.
It always protects, always trusts, always hopes, always perseveres.
Love never fails.

Corinthians 13

Now write down:

What have I found most beneficial about this chapter:

_____

_____

_____

_____

What do I need to do or in what way could I be thinking better in order to move forward:

_____

_____

_____

_____

Additional Notes:

CHAPTER SIX

BELIEVING IS SEEING
& THE VICIOUS CIRCLE

Whatever the mind of man can conceive and believe, it can achieve. Thoughts are things! And powerful things at that, when mixed with definiteness of purpose, and burning desire, can be translated into riches.

Napoleon Hill

Believing is seeing, not the other way around. When you believe your eyes will be fully opened to the wonder of your life. If you *do* keep living this in reverse you will always be living your life back to front!

Have you ever put a T-shirt or sweater on back to front by mistake? If not try it now. How uncomfortable does it feel? How silly do you look?

In reality though, we don't tend to feel silly, what we do is get angry, agitated, frustrated, sad and inert. All of these are describing words that describe certain emotions. However, I also like to think of them as the names of energies too. We tend to give ourselves 'angry' energy, 'agitated' energy and so on. This in turn has a knock on effect on our health. Such as when we are angry can give you a headache, crying too much can also do this, but more so, can make us feel empty and depressed 'what's the point' and so we create our own little vicious circle.

I do regular self development workshops and health retreats and one of the issues that we explore is what people believe to be true about themselves and also their self worth. Remember the exercise from chapter two; your thoughts = your emotions = your behaviour, and all of this will equal how you feel inside all of which reinforces **what you believe to be true about you.** This chapter is all about improving your self-worth.

Tick the following statements that are true about you.

1	I am not creative	
2	I'm too old now, my age is against me	
3	Old things are better	
4	New things are better	
5	I'd be safer not bothering	
6	Some people are just lucky	
7	Its best to just keep the peace	
8	You can't change people's beliefs	
9	I am this way because of what I have been through	
10	I deserve to be in my current situation	

11	I'm not a very confident person	
12	I'm a very private person	
13	I have to get things right	
14	I suffer from low-self esteem	
15	It's important to associate with the right kinds of people	
16	I'm not a leader	
17	It's wrong to manipulate people	
18	I'm an all or nothing person	
19	It's wrong to judge	
20	I don't deserve to be in my current situation	
21	Conflict is bad	
22	It's got to be done now	
23	They won't manage without me	

Now write down in the space provided a score you think is appropriate for you.

I am a _____ out of 10

The numbers are regularly and unfortunately heartbreaking. A very loving and mature woman gave herself a '3', I felt so sad that this is all she thought she was worth. When I asked where she had learnt this she explained that it had always been the case for her from a young child. She never felt good enough for anything, this affected her confidence and self esteem and the vicious circle continued into teenage years and adulthood.

It does not matter about the figure, you can word it any way you wish - 10 out of 10 or 100 out of 100. It is important to remember that you can change your beliefs about yourself by starting to do the opposite and 'believe' in you. If you gave yourself a '10' then absolutely fantastic, if you gave yourself anything less you may wish to consider exploring what it is that led to this lesser feeling of self worth. Alternatively you could just start immediately. Decide to change you're thinking even on one belief, otherwise you will have them forever and carrying that type of baggage is going to get tough not to mention messy. Whatever self damaging beliefs you hold about yourself that you really want to change, nip them in the bud now.

Help on How to Change Negative Beliefs:
This is an intricate one so I hope I can articulate to cover all. The first thing to do is clarify the emotions. Emotions are fantastic because they are our body's natural mechanism for letting us know how we are doing and if we are on track. If

you have done quite a bit of self development work already this may be just a case of putting pen to paper and jotting them down. Alternatively you may need to take a little more time to find out what emotions you are going through on a daily and weekly basis, which ones give you vitality and which ones do not.

The suggestion I have detailed in this chapter is to keep a journal. I regularly recommend its use for clients, and indeed I keep a journal myself when needed. There is nothing better than seeing possible issues in black and white. It is a fast track to the source of where your emotions are being generated from; who, what, when, where and how they are being facilitated. Equally, it is also a great way to get an indication of how much stress, anxiety and happiness there is in your day and what you are going to do to balance it if required.

Over the years I have learnt that clients suffering from severe anxiety, depression and other similar disorders that it is common to find it does not take much, and most things exhaust them quite quickly. Therefore this journal has been developed to require as little work possible from the client, it is time efficient with only circling or ticking required and very little writing needed.

I truly believe that doing this exercise has so many benefits. Apart from the above, it is also one of the best ways to get to the source of your beliefs about yourself and it can be applied to other things as well; religion, work ethic, expectations from relationships and so on - 'where did I learn that'. Another great by-product is that it usually uncovers the person's hidden talents and abilities. Finally, when people see how they got to the stage where they are, it can be very liberating, and really reinforces a desire to change so that they do not go through the same turmoil for the next 5, 10, 20 years. It instils confidence, integrity, courage and a desire to live life better. More often than not my client's record in this journal for a two week period, however, this depends on how chronic their symptoms are and the journal may be used for several weeks to several months.

The following describes the journey of Collette who came to me in a personal training environment to help with her exercise regime. During her initial enquiry Collette explained what she hoped to achieve but, it was very clear to me from her painfully thin physical appearance there was something wrong. We talked honestly about this and Collette explained that she had been diagnosed with anorexia nervosa. I made it clear to Collette that I could work with her physically to keep her mobile but that it would be worth considering other options to explore what was really going on. Collette agreed and it was decided to start with Life Coaching.

At the first appointment, I asked Collette to explain her diagnosis of anorexia; how it came about, who diagnosed her, what information and advice she had been currently given and how was she feeling about the diagnosis. She explained that *all* of this stemmed from her Dad leaving the family home. Also, from what Collette described to me about her condition, she had not been advised sufficiently or appropriately about this particular eating disorder and knew very little, if next to nothing at all about it. Finally, her beliefs about herself were at an all time low.

The first thing I did was educate Collette about her condition. I also had Collette explain to me where she felt she was and where she wanted to be – what did both of those places look and feel like to her? Then we set about facilitating that journey from one to the other.

We did this together with the journal being the main tool utilised for many reasons. By recording day to day life we could both see clearly the days, times, emotions and feelings that Collette was experiencing on a daily and weekly basis. We could also see how her beliefs about herself and the world around her were being created and reinforced. Finally, it helped to reveal what Collette was doing when they occurred, in other words, what coping skills she was currently using and the outcome, which generally was not healthy at all. The most important thing though, was that it very clearly gave the sources.

Whilst Collette had the unfortunate and traumatic experience of her father leaving the family and their home, not to mention the turmoil of emotion involved in something like that - it was not the source of her anorexia. An individual's name came up in the journal on quite a few occasions, whom Collette could not tolerate and would struggle to be in their company, feeling angry, embarrassed and anxious. During sessions she became visibly annoyed when she spoke about the individual to me. When we explored this, Collette spoke of an incident at work where for whatever reason that she could not explain herself, they weighed themselves. As Collette stood on the scales for her turn this particular colleague looked over her shoulder at the scales and said "I had no idea you were *that* heavy".

Collette took this information into her body on a very visceral level and *fully* believed that she was very overweight and because everything else in Collette's life regarding the family unit and so on seemed completely out of her control, what she could control was what she put in her mouth and the eating disorder took its grip.

Needless to say that once Collette worked through the fact that this was an incident that occurred outside of her body and not in her body, she readily let go of it and began to flourish in a very stunning way. Collette learned that she had the answers inside the whole time and continued to build an excellent relationship with 'herself' which had a profound effect on her confidence, self esteem and built in self worth. We used the information on Collette's journal by:

1. Exploring the daily/weekly experiences and facilitating

Collette by working through those in a safe environment and learning from them.

2. From that, we could help Collette to change her negative thinking patterns and equip her with new, healthier coping skills help her manage various situations.

3. This automatically had Collette **taking responsibility** and **control** back **of her life** and automatically making **healthy choices** for her **health and wellbeing.**

Previously Collette was literally telling herself, 'I can't look in the mirror', 'I can't go out', 'I can't deal with the stress of this', 'I can't relax', 'everything's a complete mess', 'I'm never going to meet anybody because of this'. The list of 'I can't's' went on. Of course we know from previous chapters that our thoughts create our future, you attract what you think; if you think you can, you can and if you think you can't then you can't. That is exactly what Collette had, a steady flow of that's right, 'you can't' in her life. We used several sessions to change her thinking and beliefs about herself and also to explore and visualise *exactly* what Collette could do and what she did want in her life. Collette's thought processes changed to:

'I can look in the mirror and feel great'.

'I can easily relax and let go'.

'I want to be in a loving and caring relationship'.

'I want all of my relationships to flow with respect and harmony'.

'I can go out with family and friends with ease and confidence'.

'I want my life to flow naturally, lovingly and filled with happiness and joy'.

Within two weeks other members of staff were approaching me to ask what on earth I had said or done with this girl because she looked like a completely different person, it really was an amazing transformation.

Collette achieved this positive change in her life by making the choice to do so, by taking control of her negative thinking and taking action toward her goals. It is also worth noting that whilst we have been looking at moving forward throughout this book, part of Collette's work was also letting go; letting go of the old Collette and letting go of negative patterns in order to make way for something new. That is a chapter in itself which we will be looking at in depth in chapter eight.

An example showing two days from the journal is detailed. When I work with clients this is in A4 format so you will need to re-create the journal tailoring it for you to include your own list of triggers, resulting feelings and also the seven days of the week. If the lists that I have included on the example are suitable please feel free to use them.

Personal Journal week commencing: _____   **My affirmation for the week** _____

Day:	Suspected triggers/Time of Day:	Resulted Feelings:	Action taken:	Outcome:
Mon	talking friends/w.colleague overwork/getting washed/ dressed/reading/shopping preparing meal/ social event OTHER:_____	lack of concentration/headache/ muscle ache tired/nervous/skin/problem/fear/panic/irritablefr ustrated/guilty/sad/happy/ angry / under pressure/responsible OTHER:_____		
Tue	talking friends/w.colleague overwork/getting washed/ dressed/reading/shopping preparing meal/ social event OTHER:_____	lack of concentration/headache/ muscle ache tired/nervous/skin/problem/fear/panic/irritablefr ustrated/guilty/sad/happy/ angry / under pressure/responsible OTHER:_____		

The next thing is to take action just like Collette did. Here are the steps you can now take:

The Answers are in You:
You have already looked at your worth and the fact that you are a '10', '100'! Set out **knowing** that the answers are in your system, in 'you' and describe it to yourself like Collette did:

- What is life like for me at the moment, what is it feeling like and what is it looking like?

- Where would you like it to be, what would that feel like and what would it look like?

Visualise this with as much detail as possible on a daily basis. Know and think 100% about what you do want *not* what you don't want.

Find the Answers:
Most of which you will see from your journal.

- **Who** are the people coming up in your journal, are they supportive or not, are they good for you or bad for you?

- **What** keeps coming up? What emotions are you going through on a regular basis, are they good for you or bad for you?

- **When** is it happening; morning times, late in the evening, once a week, four times a week?

- **Where** does this seem to be happening; home, work or is it when you are out socially? What environment; is the environment fine or is it a stressful, unhappy or a hostile one?

Keeping & monitoring your journal will help determine what the main **sources** of angst or unhappiness are in your life, if any.

Current Coping Skills:
- What are you saying or doing when dealing with these situations or people?

- When you communicate in this way, what is the outcome? Is it what you want and is the outcome productive?

Nine times out of ten when you look at what you are doing to cope and it *is* negative you will naturally and non-consciously start doing the opposite. When Collette and I initially started working together it was evident that she would either shut down and retreat or lose it! Through working with me on a one to one basis and completing her journal Collette reached the stage where she could recognise her warning signs accurately. The following coping strategy worked every time because it offered space, time, breathing and choice.

When Collette got hot and bothered about something I advised her to remove herself from the situation; to the staff room, photocopier and if possible completely out of the building, and she did. Collette would go to the car park and if anyone asked she was just getting a bit of air. She could literally walk into the car park, take 3 deep breaths and walk back to the office. This gave Collette's brain time to take a step back, time to have a look at how she was thinking and decide if that needed to change and also was some sort of action required; what was the best thing for her to say or do and draw on her own courage to do it. The change in attitude of others toward Collette was profound and this is just one example of a strategy you can implement that is quick and easy. When you are doing it along with everything else detailed in this book the outcome and benefits are fantastic.

Educate Yourself:

Educate yourself with what 'you' need. For example Collette was given a diagnosis she knew nothing about and therefore did not know how to deal with it. Additional to that we also addressed physical health and utilised gentle exercise to help. Others include:

- **Legal matter**, go to Citizens Advice.

- **Education** on various, go to the library or surf the net.

- **Health & Exercise**, go to your GP, local leisure or community centre.

No matter what it may be, if you need help to facilitate your situation, contact the relevant professional organisation. In this chapter I also wish to advise caution. The last three sessions with Collette were spent specifically on utilising her new found skills, but really – her thriving and glowing relationship with herself. In other words, family, friends and work colleagues were not used to her looking so good, being so positive, being decisive and being this wonderful grounded and happy person.

People around you may well struggle with the changes that they see in you, even though they are healthy and positive ones. Therefore it is important to remember that whilst working on the 'self' and changing unhelpful beliefs about yourself in order to implement healthier strategies, it may be a struggle for those around you. Do remember that not everyone has the same information as you. The truth of the matter is that the people who really care about you will be happy for you and the ones who start acting in a resentful or envious way, may need a copy of this book.

Thankfully Collette did learn that she is a '10', she is a million out of a million. You too were complete in utero, you are complete now and even when you have died and are gone from this world, you will still be a complete, wonderful person to those you have left behind.

If we think back to the start of this chapter and look at our words again. The opposite of angry could be calm, agitated could be comfortable, frustrated – relaxed, sad – happy and so on. When we are calm, comfortable, relaxed and happy with whom and where we are, the positive effect on our health is incredibly profound. You will have a lot more energy, a completely different complexion; our eyes seem to have a warm almost knowing glow in them. Can you remember having even just one of the above at some stage in your life?

- When you have been away for a few days and come back with the batteries recharged.

- Have started to take a walk now and again on your lunch break or on weekends and feel virtuous for doing something you would not normally do.

- Had a relaxation treatment such as Cranio-sacral Therapy or massage to help the body let go of any pressure or tension it has been holding and now feel completely de-stressed and re-invigorated.

Friends or family comment, 'Have you lost weight? 'You're looking very fresh this morning', 'You are very chirpy', 'You look great'. Why is that? It is not *just* the break away or the walk alone. It is because you took responsibility for yourself and when you do that, you're thinking also shifts to a brand new healthier frequency. The feelings you experience of goodness within your body and mind show physically as in your posture and also facially in your smile and in your eyes.

Apart from that it's nice, really nice to feel that way. So why not try more of it!

Another suggestion that will have a healthy affect on how you think and feel is positive affirmations. I do think the very beautiful Mother of affirmations has to be Louise Hay, her contribution to the world is phenomenal.

Louise Hay wrote a pamphlet called '*Heal Your Body*' containing a list of different bodily ailments and the probable metaphysical causes, it was later enlarged and extended into her book '*You Can Heal Your Life*' that was published in 1984. In February 2008 it was second on the New York Times miscellaneous paperback best-sellers list and today '*You Can Heal Your Life*' has been on the New York Times best-seller list with more than 50 million copies sold around the world in over 30 languages and has also has been made into a movie. You can make up your own affirmations and it can be something as simple as:

I love and approve of myself. I trust the process of life. I am safe.

However, I would highly recommend Louise Hay's book 'You Can Heal Your Life' to really help and give a better insight into the incredible power that positive affirmations can provide. The affirmations detailed on the following page are the ones I say each morning without fail.

I allow my thoughts to be free. The past is over. I am at peace.

I am a decisive person. I follow through and support myself with love.

I make my decisions based on the principles of truth and I rest securely knowing that only right action is taking place in my life.

I create firm foundations for myself and for my life. I choose my beliefs to support me joyously.

I nourish myself with love.

I release, I relax and I let go. I am safe in life. All is well in my world.

Everything we would ever need to become rich and powerful and sophisticated is within our reach. The major reason that so few take advantage of all that we have is simply neglect.
Jim Rohn

And these are my final words on negative beliefs about yourself and creating a vicious circle through lack of taking responsibility. Why would you neglect yourself any longer?

Now write down:

What have I found most beneficial about this chapter:

_____

_____

_____

_____

What do I need to do or in what way could I be thinking better in order to move forward:

_____

_____

_____

_____

Additional Notes:

Winner of the Choral Speech Festival

My 'Connect' Radio Show

Lady in Red

I passed
my exams!

What a
celebration!

Beyond Business Awards - looking good!

After all that 'achieving' my first well deserved holiday in 9 years

The Great
Blasket Islands

Perfect start to
my day!

*Irish Children's
Program - fantastic*

*A favourite of
mine*

My Sanctuary

One of the best times ever

Grotta Palazzese, Polignano A Mare

*Casalini
'Festival of the
Vine'*

CHAPTER SEVEN

YOUR DREAMS & THE ROSE WITHIN

Sometimes I do wake up in the mornings and feel like I've just had the most incredible dream. I've just dreamt my life.
Richard Branson

I quote the previous chapter 'Believing *is* Seeing'. When we believe in our dreams and our spirit we capture our lives, the lives that deep, deep inside - we want to live. *It is* the felt sense that follows you all of your life, and it will always be fighting to get out. A life that you will look back on and feel proud of, relaxed about and excited at what you have achieved and what you have produced – y*our purpose.*

I believe 100% that our dreams are our *real* lives, the difficulty is we don't believe it. Most people set out thinking that there is no point, their dreams cannot possibly become reality. Those dreams then become the tragedy that life is and the person becomes a victim suffering this cruel, cruel life. Of course not all people accept the victim role, 'this is it for me - one big tragedy after another'. Some people do something about it and **so can you**.

If you want more, you have to require more from yourself.
Dr Phil

There are limitless examples of 'rags to riches' stories that started back as far as Cinderella! Movies such as Rocky, Trading Places, The Pursuit of Happiness and Slumdog Millionaire not to mention the incredible story of J.K Rowling *all* illustrating that really and truly –

ANYTHING IS POSSIBLE.

But, it is not just about 'rags to riches' from a monetary point of view but what is important to you or you would like to do more of in your life; getting more time for a hobby, go on a holiday, move home. What is the big dream for you or what is it that is of great importance? What is it that you are going to be so enthused and excited about that it makes you get out of bed and make a start, make a phone call – whatever it is that starts to turn the dream or important issue to reality!

The following demonstrates just how incredible the outcome *can* be from what most people would consider impossible circumstances for any change at all.

Dan M. "Buck" Brannaman is a horse trainer and leading practitioner within the field of natural horsemanship. Buck had an extremely difficult childhood suffering shocking abuse at the hands of his father to the extent that he and his brother spent a number of years in foster care placements. A skilled Trick Roper and included in the Guinness Book of Records for his incredible achievements Buck performed rope tricks in television commercials since he was six years old but Buck explains at that time "my dad gave us the choice of practicing roping tricks or getting whipped".

Buck took solace in horses and learned from his own experiences to look at a situation from the point of view of the horse. "I've started horses since I was 12 years old and have been bit, kicked, bucked off and run over. I've tried every physical means to contain my horse in an effort to keep from getting myself killed. I started to realize that things would come much easier for me once I learned *why* a horse does what he does. "He later used these experiences in his career as a horse trainer recognizing in difficult animals the same fear and hostile reactions he remembered from his own childhood. "Abused horses are like abused children, they trust no one and expect the worst. But patience, leadership, compassion and firmness can help them overcome their pasts."

In recent years, Buck has become a motivational speaker for groups outside of the horse world, frequently describing the connection between animal abuse and abuse of children and other human beings. "For me these principles are really about life," says Buck, "about living your life so that you're not making war with the horse or with other people. Horses are incredibly forgiving, they fill in places we're not capable of filling ourselves. They've given people a new hope, a new lease on life. A horse really wants to please you, to get along."

Buck was also one of the primary individuals who inspired the character of Tom Booker in the Nicholas Evans novel *The Horse Whisperer* and was the lead equine consultant for the film. Though the book itself was a work of fiction Evans himself said "Others have falsely claimed to be the inspiration for Tom Booker in The Horse Whisperer. The one who truly inspired me was Buck Brannaman. His skill, understanding and his gentle, loving heart have parted the clouds for countless troubled creatures. Buck is the Zen master of the horse world". A documentary about him called 'Buck', won the U.S. Documentary Audience Award at the 2011 Sundance Film Festival and I would highly recommend that you get a copy to watch, it truly is inspirational as is the man himself.

Dave featured in the papers in 2008. A father aged 50 from West Bromwich UK, he is famous for running seven marathons on seven continents in seven days.

Starting in the Falkland Islands in the South Atlantic on 7 April 2008, Dave and his running partner Malcolm Carr then moved onto Rio, Santiago the capital of Chile, Los Angeles in

California, Sydney, Dubai and Nairobi before returning to Europe and completing the daunting challenge by running the London Marathon on 13 April 2008. What made the seven marathons on seven continents such a spectacular feat? Dave is blind.

An influential female that most people around the world will know of is **Oprah Winfrey**. I personally was not aware of just how traumatic her upbringing was. Oprah was born into poverty in rural Mississippi to a teenage single mother and later raised in inner-city Milwaukee where she experienced considerable hardship during childhood. It was only when she got a job in radio whilst still in high school that life began to improve. Oprah's emotional ad-lib delivery eventually got her transferred to the daytime talk show arena and after boosting a third-rated local Chicago talk show to first place she launched her own production company and became internationally syndicated. It was actually on her own show in November 1986 on sexual abuse victims and their molesters that Oprah then revealed she herself was raped by a relative when she was just 9 years old and that she became pregnant at 14 but her son died in infancy.

Quoted at the start of chapter two 'It doesn't matter who you are, where you come from. The ability to triumph begins with you'. True to her own words Oprah Winfrey is now the multiple-Emmy Award winning host of The Oprah Winfrey

Show the highest-rated talk show in the history of television. She is also an influential book critic, Academy Award-nominated actress and magazine publisher. Oprah Winfrey is now one of Americas most wealthy and successful women, ranked the richest African American of the 20th century, the most philanthropic African American of all time and the world's only black billionaire for three straight years. She is also according to some the most influential woman in the world!

Mary Byrne was born in Ballyfermot in Dublin in November 1959. Up until 2010 Mary was a single Mum of a 23 year old daughter and worked on the check outs at her local Tesco store. She said if 'X factor' ever came to Dublin she would definitely have a go. It did. Her niece posted her application and the rest is history.

Whilst it was Matt Cardle who won the competition Mary's popularity and success soared and within months released her own album 'Mine & Yours' which debuted at number one in Ireland immediately.

When asked about advice to others who are older and feel they missed their dream Mary said 'Go live it. You've still got years left in you, so when you die, at least you had a good time doing it.' Mary ended the interview by saying 'When you get to this age, if you don't enjoy life, you may as well just lay down and die'.

Paulo Coelho is a novelist and lyricist. His father was an engineer and his mother a home-maker. As a teenager Paulo wanted to become a writer and when he told his mother she responded with "My dear, your father is an engineer, he's a logical, reasonable man with a very clear vision of the world, do you actually know what it means to be a writer?"

At 17 Paulo's opposition to follow the traditional path led to his parents committing him to a mental institution from which he escaped several times before being released at the age of 20. Paulo later said 'It wasn't that they wanted to hurt me, but they didn't know what to do, they did not do that to destroy me, they did that to save me'.

In 1987 Coelho published *The Alchemist* which went on to sell more than 65 million copies becoming one of the best-selling books in history and has been translated into more than 67 languages.

In April 2008 Paulo Coelho had a new Guinness World Record to his credit, the 2009 Guinness World Record for the Most Translated Living Author with William Shakespeare as the Most Translated Author of all time.

Archie Barton. This little boy featured in the paper in July 2009, not for how much money he earned or an empire he built but his first steps to rebuilding his life after being struck down with meningitis.

This courageous little child was just 18 months old he had both legs amputated after his body was ravaged by septicaemia. His fingers had to be partially or entirely removed after they turned black and he also lost most of his eyesight. After 18months of agonising hospital procedures for Archie and his family they got a breakthrough with new lightweight legs. As soon as Archie got his £12,500.00 bionic legs in his favourite colour red he was off! His Mum explained that he can't wait to get up in the morning to get them on and he'll shout 'Click-click me in Mummy' and went on to say, he is like a new boy and is so much happier, he never moans'. You can read Archie's full story at archiesstory.co.uk.

The miracles that take place in life are created by you. The people detailed above are heroes and they all have one thing in common:

They rose to the challenges of life they faced.
They did not let past life experience define who they are.
They created their own miracle.

We all have an impact on the world dependent on what you see out of your eyes, they are your windows to the world, your world.

It doesn't matter what you do; if you run a business empire you impact the world, if you do voluntary work you affect the world, if you become an alcoholic you have an impact on the world and even if you become a recluse, you affect the world.

LIFE IS A CHALLENGE NOT A TRAGEDY
YOUR PAST DOES NOT DEFINE WHO YOU ARE OR
WHAT THE OUTCOME WILL BE.

People do go through horrendous tragedy, and life at times is far from easy. People like little Archie, others with terminal illness who are battling on with the most amazing strength and courage. So what is it? What is it that you are dying of that is making you want to give up? We have a choice, just as little Archie did and so do you.

Quite regularly a client will say to me "Sinead, I just don't know where to start" which is another reason I wrote this book. In your case reading now, you are already making in-roads from the previous chapters you have been reading and all of the exercises you have been 'actively' doing to move your life forward. I am now going to share another incredibly powerful and useful tool. I do this exercise each year to help me re-assess and focus in on my morals, values and desires. The week coming up to Christmas I print off three pages, which are headed with:

The Things I did not like about _____
The Things I Really Enjoyed about _____
What I am Going to Achieve in _____

The blank line in the first two titles is where I insert the year that has just passed and in the final title I insert the coming year. I carry the lists with me to work and also have them in and around my home when I am there so that they will catch my eye. Over the remainder of Christmas and into the New Year I jot down the things that will eventually create my list on each page. Each of the pages are numbered from 1-10, however, you can list as little or more if you like.

This is an exceptionally good exercise that helps you acknowledge some of the things/incidents from the previous year that you did not like. What seems to happen when you perform the physical act of writing them down, is that you non-consciously will let them go. The things you enjoyed you will non-consciously do more of which becomes apparent when you go to do the lists again the following year. Finally, the things you wish to achieve in the coming year, you will do non-consciously. Again the act of physically writing what you wish to achieve seems to imprint it in your being and sends that energy deep into your body and mind and out into the universe. I have had maybe five things that I wish to achieve and maybe the following year I have done four out of that five, I feel this is outstanding. In which case the one that I missed will go on my list for the following year if it is genuinely something I 'still' wish to achieve.

The lists are included on the following pages for you to use and although I normally do this exercise at the start of each year there was one year that I did not do it until May but I still found it beneficial. I have never known this exercise to fail.

THINGS **I AM GOING TO ACHIEVE IN** _____

1. _____

2. _____

3. _____

4. _____

5. _____

6. _____

7. _____

8. _____

9. _____

10. _____

THINGS **I REALLY ENJOYED ABOUT** _____

1._____

2._____

3._____

4._____

5._____

6._____

7._____

8._____

9._____

10._____

THINGS **I DID NOT LIKE IN** _____

1._____

2._____

3._____

4._____

5._____

6._____

7._____

8._____

9._____

10._____

It is worth noting that just writing these lists does not mean that's you done. They are done collectively with all of the other guidance in this book and of course, taking action.

I would also like to look at your dreams from another angle by seeing you, your life and dreams as a rose bush. Again, trust me, there is a point here!

Several years ago I was invited to do a motivational seminar to a group with disabilities that ranged from cerebral palsy to learning difficulties. I asked the group to think of a young rose bush that had just buds with no flower, and in not knowing, would they stamp it out, crush it or even throw it away 'You're not a rose bush, you don't have any roses!'. They of course said 'no'. I asked what they would do. They explained collectively that they would feed it with water and food, give it sunlight, some said they would talk to it, but the general consensus was that they would tend to and look after it and watch out for the roses coming into bloom. **And so it is with you**.

Remember:

- Feed your dreams like a rose bush with the right ingredients; places, people, education and so on. Visualise them becoming reality.

- Give your mind and body the light it needs; relax from time to time, walk in the park, read a book, soak in a bath, fresh air and light.

- Talk and just 'be' with yourself and clarify; what do I need, what do I like, what are my dreams, what things can I do to begin my dreams and then allow the world to conspire to help you.

- If there has been a trauma/tragedy for you, seek out the relevant help that you need to help resolve it for you.

Your life begins to unfold without you even realising into the most beautiful rose in full bloom. Having talked earlier about the group I worked with and how I used the analogy of a rose, I couldn't believe it when I came across this writing in a St Martin booklet a few years later, I thought it would be a nice one to share.

The Rose Within

A certain man planted a rose and watered it faithfully and before it blossomed he examined it. He saw the bud that would soon blossom and also the thorns. And he thought, "How can any beautiful flower come from a plant burdened with so many sharp thorns?" Saddened by this thought, he neglected to water the rose, and before it was ready to bloom, it died.

So it is with many people. Within every soul there is a rose. The God-like qualities planted in us at birth grow amid the thorns of our faults. Many of us look at ourselves and see only the thorns, the defects. We despair, thinking that nothing good

116

can possibly come from us. We neglect to water the good within us, and eventually it dies. We never realise our potential.

Some people do not see the rose within themselves; someone else must show it to them. One of the greatest gifts a person can possess is to be able to reach past the thorns and find the rose within others. This is the characteristic of love, to look at a person, and knowing his faults, recognise the nobility in his soul, and help him realise that he can overcome his faults. If we show him the rose, he will conquer the thorns. Then will he blossom, blooming forth thirty, sixty, a hundred fold as it is given to him.

Our duty in this world is to help others by showing them their roses and not their thorns. Only then can we achieve the love we should feel for each other; only then can we bloom in our own garden.
Author Unknown

The final few points I would like to make in this chapter is the **<u>fact</u>** that anything is possible and that every dream, wish or desire starts somewhere and usually quite small, there are endless examples. Your dreams or goals are going to require effort. It could be weeks, months or years of sticking with it but even Alice had to fall down a big hole and land on her backside before she got to Wonderland!

I've tried to think of an example of duration that would be as universal as I could get and the band U2 came to mind. The band formed way back in 1976 at Mount Temple Comprehensive School when they were only teenagers and every member had very limited musical proficiency. It took four years before they got signed by Island Records when they released their debut album *Boy*. It was in the mid-1980s that they became an international act, but Bono and the rest of the band didn't get the big break 'the dream' that would seriously put them on the map until 1987 when they released their breakthrough album *The Joshua Tree* – 11 years hard, hard graft!

You have to stick with it and put the effort in, **purposeful effort** which is the physical and mental effort directed at doing or making something happen. Yes, it may be a lot of hard work but *it is* worth it. Completing the three lists each year is just another way of bringing your hopes and dreams to the fore. Remember you also have your structured personal plan back in chapter four and journal in chapter six and if you figure out other ways of getting 'you' up and running with whatever it is you wish to achieve and it really works for you then great.

My point here on dreams and goals is that if they are not written down and planned for they will be like seeds without soil or water or love! Martin Luther King said, 'You don't have to see the whole staircase, just take the first step'. I hope that you do.

Now write down:

What have I found most beneficial about this chapter:

_____

_____

_____

_____

What do I need to do or in what way could I be thinking better in order to move forward:

_____

_____

_____

_____

Additional Notes:

CHAPTER EIGHT

FORGIVE

There are two levels to your pain: the pain that you create now, and the pain from the past that still lives on in your mind and body. Ceasing to create pain in the present and dissolving past pain - this is what I want to talk about now.

Eckhart Tolle

'Letting go' was touched on very briefly in chapter six and can also be described another way: **forgive**. Whether that is forgiving others is up to you, my concern here, is forgiving yourself and letting go of your 'old' self, dissolving past pain.

If you have got to this chapter you are ready to let go or at least are making massive in-roads into doing so. For the simple reason, you are not the same person now that you were before you read chapter seven, you were not the same person after reading chapter six and so on. You have been evolving at each chapter and taking on board beautiful new information. So, before the filters clog up we let go, for fresh, healthier input.

In order to begin forgiveness and help dissolve past

pain, we are going to look at what is still living on in your mind and body and also your environment. As always this is individual. Some people feel the need to let go by processing information and coming to some sort of conclusion themselves before they feel they can forgive. Others feel you need to forgive and then let go. There is no right or wrong way, if it works for you and gets the results you need to move forward that is the result we are after.

This chapter could be taxing for you both physically and mentally because when you think about letting go or forgiving, you may well also be reminded of the incident or person involved that caused the hurt and pain. For this reason I decided to look at the environment first. This is a good way to adjust and become a little more comfortable with even thinking about any pain that is still living within and around you. What we need here is:

- Reduced distress
- Freedom of mind
- Unshackle yourself
- Breathe easy
- Open your senses
- Move forward now
- Become liberated with yourself

Looking at your environment can be emotional but it can also be incredibly therapeutic and good fun. We are going to get rid of a lot *or* all of your baggage by literally throwing half of it out! I want there to be no misunderstanding, 'tidying up' is not the same as a heart to heart with personal items and yourself. Take a few minutes now and wherever you are sitting look around or simply visualise a person, place or thing that has negatively affected you. How do you feel about the thoughts coming to your mind? Write them down.

1. Is what you are seeing making you **smile** and bringing warmth, or is it upsetting; sadness, hurt, anger or sense of loss?

---

2. Why are you experiencing these thoughts and emotions about what you see?

---

3. What other places or rooms in your home help you **reflect**? Where do you go to do that? If you don't know, write that down.

Now, Mr, Miss or Mrs Reader reading this book - think about it. You not only have a lot going on in your mind you also have it all around you, reminding you of your past, present and possible future. Whether you like it or not, your depression, stress, anxiety, IBS, lethargy, back pain and so on is not helped *at all* by being overwhelmed with unnecessary 'stuff'. Even if you do not agree with the above one thing is fact - if you need a very good reason to do this particular exercise:

AFTER YOU DO, YOU WILL FEEL BETTER.

You will be less stressed because you can now find things easily enough. More space to move both physically and emotionally. You won't have to be embarrassed by your mess (we've all been there at some stage!) and, you could cut future cleaning time. Look at all of the wonderful potential benefits.

Practical benefits:

✓ Kitchens & Bathrooms will be free from expired food, cosmetics and appliances you no longer need or use; hair tongs, juicers, bread maker etc creating space.

✓ Furniture will be used for its intended purpose i.e. the dining room table can be used for meal times not as a dumping ground for things that need to be put away.

✓ Sentimental items such as photographs and keepsakes will be organised and displayed in such a way that you can readily view them.

- ✓ Children's toys and clothes will have a home of their own which can help make sorting clothes, washing, drying and ironing as time efficient as possible.

- ✓ You will have systems set in place to recycle easily, everything from newspapers to glass.

- ✓ Have filing systems in place for household paperwork. This allows you to easily access individual bills when required and allows you to 'action' post at regular intervals.

- ✓ Clothes & shoes will be kept in the appropriate places i.e. wardrobes, drawers or shoe stacking units.

- ✓ Your keys and other objects such as mobile phones, gloves and umbrellas will all have a home.

- ✓ You can have a system in place to categorise CD's & DVD's in suitable storage so that they are easily accessible.

- ✓ Surfaces around your home; chairs, tables and stairs will be free from clutter.

- ✓ You will be able to access all areas of your home inside and out; hallway, bedrooms and so on.

- ✓ Cleaning will be easier and quicker.

Health benefits:

✓ You will sleep better in a clean and tidy environment.

✓ You will feel more energised to start projects and carry them through to the end.

✓ You will feel better equipped to deal with life on a day to day basis.

✓ You will have more time to pursue hobbies and outside interests.

✓ Your general health may improve, less colds and flu each year.

✓ You will be equipped to part with past items more readily that can keep you stuck.

Finally, there may even be the opportunity to earn additional cash. A few years ago I had client who wanted to raise petrol money and I advised a car book sale. We both did a complete de-clutter and went along to my local car boot the following Sunday. Sarah was delighted when she cashed up at the end of the day to discover she had made just over £150.00 selling jewellery, bags and clothes. The highest selling item was her old jigsaw puzzles, she had quite a few and they all sold.

The following are the steps for your de-clutter. I would stress the need to consider time involved. Have you ever gone looking for something and when you found it started looking at something else and something else? I called to my parent's home for some paperwork I had stored in the attic and came across a bag of old photographs and diaries. I was there pretty much the whole day reminiscing. When I de-clutter I set aside *that* time, a full Saturday or Sunday with as little interruption as possible. It leaves sufficient time to take a break for a cup of tea and regular smaller breaks if needed.

PLAN:

Identify what cluttered areas cause you the most frustration and then jot down what is required to resolve it. It could be anything from clearing out one drawer, setting up a filing system for paperwork or a clothes clear-out. If you don't need the jotting down go ahead and get started.

DE-CLUTTER = DE-STRESS:

Emotions can affect how we de-clutter in a big way and fall into many categories. Here are a few:

What you are **definitely keeping:**	These are items that have nothing but happy memories such as clothing you always wear and feel comfort from – the things that make you smile.
What you are **unsure of** and will maybe store for a while:	These items generate comfort in a different way. Like keeping an old flame alive or belongings from a loved one who has since passed away. Usually these are the things you want to de-clutter but emotion & memory will just not allow it, and that's ok.
What you would like to take to a **second hand store/car boot:**	These are the things we can let go of happily. We've loved them, lost them and embraced the lessons/experience from them in a healthy way and now someone else can benefit from them.
What you are **getting rid** of:	The 'eye sores'. You would think these would be the ones I would say "yip, get rid, get it out". No. I suggest you pause and explore. Why does it bug me? Why do I think it's an eyesore? What emotion do I get when I think of this? Embrace; is there a hidden lesson here for me? *THEN* de-clutter and **let it go.**

ORGANISE IT:

✓ Look at what space you now have available and the best way to use it.

✓ Arrange furniture and accessories how you want them for easy access and easy living.

✓ Dispose of any large pieces that are rarely used. For example replace an unused large bed by investing in a futon for occasional visitors.

✓ Invest in multi-storage units where needed or use the storage you have in a more effective way.

✓ Organise everything you have done; label boxes to be stored in the attic/garage, put like for like together in your clothing wardrobe and so on.

MAINTAIN IT:

Set rules at home. For example, if you use something you also put it back in its home *after* use, coats are hung up and not left on the sofa or dining table and children put away their toys properly. Continue and encourage others, especially children to keep it going, aim for a clean and tidy environment together.

Wallowing in the past may be good literature
As wisdom, it's hopeless.
Aldous Huxley

REFLECT:

Letting go of items can be tough, but once you make a start it can be liberating and generate a sense of freedom and you can feel 'lighter'. The more often you do this *properly*, the more you will find that you intuitively grasp what your belongings and people who have entered your life mean for you and why they came into your life in the first place. It also makes you more aware for the future.

Whether you have been letting go of negative thoughts that have been taking up too much brain space, or clearing a cabinet full of old bank statements that are a reminder of a difficult financial time for you, take the time to reflect. This can help you move towards letting go fully by immediately or gradually allowing any residue of memory of those negative or difficult times in your life, to lift out of your body and mind. Complete the following questions.

➢ When you were letting go of your 'stuff', what came up for you?

_____

_____

➤ What do you feel you have achieved?

_____

_____

_____

➤ How can you apply this to other areas of your life?

_____

_____

_____

➤ Describe how you are feeling now?

_____

_____

_____

REST:

Have a cup of tea, soak in the bath or sit in the garden. Whatever you decide, give yourself the space you need and just be good to yourself.

Most of us, when we feel out of sorts, are reluctant to acknowledge the part which mental trouble is playing in our dissatisfaction and discomfort. We feel that we are ourselves responsible for any sort of mental or emotional failure; and so, to save our pride, we almost unconsciously seek to assign the whole blame to our liver, or our digestion, or to some physiological cause which we assume to be outside our control. The functioning of our bodies is, in fact, however, largely dependent on the agreeably varied exercise of our emotions. The too long persistence of any emotional state which does not find an outlet inaction, leads to a state of tension which inevitably disturbs our unconscious physiological processes.
Dr Harry Roberts

Some of the common threads throughout this book being mentioned again; exercise of the emotions and the importance of finding an outlet by taking action which is what you have just done. Clients who do this exercise from start to finish find it very beneficial. Some describe that they just feel much better in themselves and others tell me how they ended up having a complete clear-out of the whole house!

Big pat on the back.

In the Bible it says they asked Jesus how many times you should forgive, and he said 70 times 7. Well, I want you all to know that I'm keeping a chart.
Hillary Rodham Clinton

Forgiveness is such a powerful and incredibly tricky subject. I think this is because when someone causes deep, deep hurt, it may feel or just is not possible to even conceive the idea of forgiving them and it can take a long time before we do. We have looked at your environment and now I am going to help you cease creating further pain in the present, by forgiving your past.

There is serious atrocity and conflict continuing throughout the world as you read this; acts of violence, drug trafficking, human trafficking, suicide and sexual abuse to name just a few. We *all* experience it right down to the smaller conflicts in our own lives; disagreements at home, arguments with family, bad fall-outs with friends and even with our children, no matter the age. The outcome of which is usually heightened emotions; anger, anguish, anxiety, guilt, sadness, shame and worry about the whole situation, whatever it was that happened. I really do think when the dust settles one of the things we continue to struggle with well after the event is over, is the inability to forgive ourselves for the role we played.

Gandhi, Mandela and all the greats say that the only person you can really change is yourself and that is the one I would like to talk about now. The disagreements we have with ourselves in our own minds, the guilt from our past actions that we cannot let go of, the hurt caused to us by others that we are so disappointed in, leaves within us massive confusion and often a destructive power that continues to cause deep pain and hurt in our lives in the present. I am not attempting to sort out world atrocity and conflict, I am not even asking you to forgive some else. What I am asking you to consider is forgiving yourself.

IT WILL MAKE YOUR WORLD A BETTER PLACE.

I truly believe that you know yourself; the various incidents in your life that you are deeply unhappy about, things you could have handled better, things you said that you wish to goodness you had not. What is in the past *is* in the past and you cannot change that. This is about equipping you *now* for the future.

You may not be familiar with Francois-Marie Arouet (1694-1778) but with his pen name 'Voltaire'. He was a great French enlightenment writer, essayist and philosopher known for his wit and defence of civil liberties including both freedom of religion and free trade. Voltaire was a prolific writer and produced works in pretty much every literary form. I love the following quote, it is beautiful and helps remind me of how fragile we are and also to just give ourselves a break from time to time.

No snowflake in an avalanche ever feels responsible.
Voltaire

You are only responsible for one person's thoughts, actions and words, that of yourself. So how do you forgive yourself? You do this by **making peace with yourself**. If you have been actively participating whilst reading this book, completing the various exercises and taking action you have been achieving so much and making peace with yourself already. The following is a fantastic exercise and remember, our bodies *listen* to what we tell it so the following sentences need to be said out loud:

Forgiving Affirmations

"By making peace with myself I am forgiving 'me'. This has a powerful positive affect on my mind, body and emotions"

"By choosing to forgive myself now, I am helping to reduce the confusion in my life"

"By forgive myself, I am leaving room for happier relationships"

"Forgiving myself instils personal respect and confidence within me"

"I have the courage to forgive myself because I can"

It is important to keep doing this exercise to help you make peace more and more, life is too short to spend another second at war with yourself.

The next exercise can help when dealing with smaller conflicts. This could be someone at work that you struggle with or an argument that you know is silly, but you do not know how to resolve it. The following questions are a good start to help you explore the situation in a healthy way and depending on what the issue is, will depend on what questions are applicable.

- What aspect of this person's personality causes you the difficulty? *Or* what is it about this situation that is causing you difficulty?

  _____

  _____

- What does that tell you about you?

  _____

  _____

- What strategy have you used so far to help resolve your feelings?

  _____

  _____

- Has this been effective?

  _____

  _____

- What needs to happen in order to resolve this for you?

  _____

  _____

- What small change could you make in your behaviour that could have a *good* impact?

  _____

  _____

If you feel that the person or issue is too overwhelming then it is no longer a small conflict and you may need to seek professional help in order to resolve it fully and in a healthy way.

The following is a guide on dealing with forgiveness, should that be working on forgiving yourself or others that may help you in the future. They are a good mix, some you may get motivation from and others may not apply to you at all. Take what you need.

LISTEN:

You can't change what you don't acknowledge.
Dr Phil

Set aside time in a place you can go to and really 'listen' to yourself and acknowledge past hurts. Allow your ears to hear it all; blame, insults, anger, fear, guilt and remorse. Say or should everything you want without stopping - let it all out.

COURAGE:

Courage is the most important of all the virtues because without courage, you can't practice any other virtue consistently.
Maya Angelou

Resolving an issue takes a lot of courage because it means being emotionally vulnerable, doing something you might be scared of. Practice risking 'rejection' in small things. For example try smiling at someone, if they don't smile back you'll get over it, but try to stay in touch with that feeling and build on it.

BE CREATIVE:

Creativity involves breaking out of established patterns in order to look at things in a different way.
Edward de Bono

You may feel that you have tried all the obvious things and none of them worked. Use your imagination, do some brainstorming and open-ended thinking <u>without barriers</u>. For example, if there is something you really want to resolve what could you do to start the conversation? What could you do to show you really want to make up? What could you do to deal with the underlying issues? What is the most beautiful way I can handle this? When the brain starts searching for the answers, jot them down.

INSPIRE OTHERS:

We make a living by what we get, but we make a life by what we give.
Winston Churchill

Being a role model and the ability to listen and remain non-judgemental is one of the most powerful ways that you help lift and inspire others. When someone feels comfortable enough to share their story with you of how they feel about arguments, hurts or disappointments that have happened, can support and help them to make difficult but maybe necessary choices for their future.

CHOICE:

We who lived in the concentration camps can remember the men who walked through the huts comforting others, giving away their last piece of bread. They may have been few in

number but they offer sufficient proof that everything can be taken away from a man but one thing, the last of the human freedoms – to choose one's attitude in any given set of circumstances, to choose one's own way.
Victor Frankl

There is no explaining needed here. What incredible words in the face of extreme adversity.

TAKE A RISK:

Do not wait; the time will never be 'just right'. Start where you stand, and work with whatever tools you may have at your command, and better tools will be found as you go along.
Napoleon Hill

Reach out, pick up the phone, send that e-mail and just do it. There will never be a perfect moment and if you speak from your heart about what you feel you lose nothing and may even gain something priceless.

FEAST:

If you can't feed a hundred people then feed just one.
Mother Teresa

Take scones or muffins into the office, surprise your neighbour with biscuits or invite someone you are having difficulty with to dinner. Serve a soup, stew or curry, something that can be placed in a big pot to be shared and give each other space and time to talk during the meal.

BE INCLUSIVE:

If you judge people, you have no time to love them.
Mother Teresa

Sustainable change is made when *everyone* is involved in it, involved in the making peace or the forgiving process.

I would now like to share with you the true story of how an incredible individual dealt with a heinous crime committed against her and humanity. Reading about another's experience can be inspirational and help bring about perspective regarding our own situations. Gill was the last person to be rescued from her train in the London bombings and has worked ever since as a passionate Peace Activist. The following is Gill's account.

"We have such incredible ability and power to make choices, to make a positive difference and to leave the world better off than when we entered. For me, I wasn't given a choice when a young man detonated his bomb in the train carriage I was travelling in BUT I did have a choice in how I wanted to react, how I wanted to express my disbelief, anger and sadness at what he had done to me and to so many who were my fellow commuters.

It wasn't difficult to make the choices that I did. I instinctively wanted to celebrate the fact that I survived, that I could experience all that being alive offered. My memories were not of the blast and its trauma, it was of the unconditional love that was given to me by all those who fought so hard to save me, the people who held my hand tightly. There were many who risked their own lives to save mine, however they did so not knowing me, it simply didn't matter who I was, what I believed, how much money I had – to them I was a precious human life.

My peace is in my heart. My peace is the beaming smile on my face. My peace is the embrace that I can share with those I love. My peace is knowing that I can contribute to the world. My peace is feeling grateful and appreciative for every day that I am here. My peace is completely understanding that two 'Wrongs' can't make it 'Right'."

Gill Hicks

Just like Richard Moore's story that was described in chapter five, again Gill reinforces to us the incredible power we have when we have a choice. It was Mohandas K. Gandhi who said "The weak can never forgive, forgiveness is the attribute of the strong".

This chapter is all about forgiveness and I hope it makes a positive contribution to your life. Be strong and be forgiving. I leave you with an excerpt from 'Life Lessons' by Elizabeth Kubler-Ross and David Kessler. Every individual or home should have a copy of this book, order your copy as soon as possible.

"We need to forgive so that we can live whole lives. Forgiveness is the way to heal our hurts and wounds, it's how we reconnect with others and ourselves. We have all been hurt—we didn't deserve the pain, but were wounded nonetheless. And, if truth be told, we have almost certainly hurt others. The problem isn't that hurt happens, it's that we can't or won't forget it. This is the hurt that keeps on hurting. We go through life accumulating these hurts; we have no training or guidance in how to let them go. This is where forgiveness comes in.
We have a choice to live in forgiveness or unforgiveness".
Elizabeth Kubler-Ross

Now write down:

What have I found most beneficial about this chapter:

_____

_____

_____

_____

What do I need to do or in what way could I be thinking better in order to move forward:

_____

_____

_____

_____

Additonal Notes:

CHAPTER 9

TAKE THE RISK

Yes, risk taking is inherently failure-prone.
Otherwise, it would be called sure-thing-taking.
Tim McMahon

We talked loosely in earlier chapters of this book that most people will get around seventy-five years, and if that is the case for most of us then why not do something with it? There are several reasons why we do not, for example neglect as mentioned at the tail end of chapter six. But 'the biggy' is our old faithful that never leaves us - **'fear'**.

Fear of living, fear of taking a risk because it may not work out. However, there is always the flip side of this – what if it is the best risk you have ever taken in the world? I have found through experience that I only ever regretted the things I did not do because I was never going to know what the outcome could have been, at least if I tried, I would have the experience and know if it was good or not. We are scared, and think there are things we cannot possibly do because of the environment we are in and that we cannot change the environment. However the changes that matter the most are more often than not, changes in our perception rather than changes in the world outside of us. We *can* change the way we perceive our environment and the world in a heartbeat. Risks come in many forms so here are just a few mixed in with all of that 'fear' we play over and over again in our minds:

Changing your occupation	What if I don't like it? What if it comes down to it and I can't do the job? What if it all goes wrong? What if I'm left with financial burden?
Performing a Challenging feat	What if the day arrives and I'm too frightened to do it? What if I fail? What if I don't do it right?
Asking someone out on a date	What if they say no? What if I'm rejected? What if I fail?
Relationships	I'm afraid of getting hurt, I will only hurt them and so on. I can't leave, they'll be devastated or what if I don't meet anyone else?
Standing up for something you firmly believe in	I don't know, it's going against society, it means I won't fit in anymore. I'm afraid of having a different opinion, I'm afraid nobody will listen.
Forgiveness	If I forgive them they'll just do it again?

Of course the risks we are discussing are not about getting into a cage with a lion just for the laugh of it. We are talking about our day to day struggles, future struggles or wanting to take a risk to make a particular dream become reality. Also, the risks we are prepared to take come down to the individual and will more than likely change throughout life. For example asking a female or male out on a date may not scare you as much or have the same 'fear' hold over you now as it would have when you were only fifteen or sixteen years old. Then, if we look at pretty massive risk, Chris Evans springs to my mind.

I watched an interview of him on television where he detailed to the interviewer the massive risks involved about 'that deal'. Sir Richard Branson had decided to reduce his media holding and began talks to sell his radio station to Capital Radio in a deal that would have given him 10% of the holding company Capital Group. When it became public knowledge Chris Evans, who was currently employed at the station did not want to work for Capital and decided to buy them out.

With literally minutes left on the clock and the assistance of investors, not to mention every last penny that he had, Ginger Media Group, owned by Chris Evans, bought Virgin Radio from Branson for £85 million, he was 30 years old. It was a massive risk that paid off and in March 2000 Chris Evans agreed the sale of Ginger Media Group to SMG Plc for a staggering £225 million.

I am not suggesting for a second that you go out and sell your home to buy a franchise of some sort in the hope that it pays off well. What I do want to help with or share, is how do we get *more comfortable* with starting or taking more of a risk? All of the people you admire, whether that is your parents, sports personalities, spiritualists or musicians have *learnt* everything they know by repeatedly practicing their skill until it becomes a habit.

YOU ARE NO DIFFERENT.

You learnt how to walk, talk, read, write, dance, ride a bike and drive a car - the list is endless. If we take the car as an example. You learnt how to drive by observing your driving instructor and after copying him/her you then practiced and practiced until you could drive, reverse, tackle a roundabout, emergency stop and so on. So how do you get more comfortable with taking a risk?

YOU PRACTICE.
START TAKING A RISK EVERY DAY.

If the people you admire had listened to all of the negativity or been too scared to take a chance, where would they be and how different would their lives be now? If I had listened to all of my fears and my inner critic I probably would not have done very much, I certainly would not have written this book and sadly it is such a big thing for millions of people. I have worked with clients and groups where their fears are so great it almost paralyses them to the point where some people will not leave their homes. You may have been dealing with some of your own fears whilst reading this book and taking 'mini' risks and obviously this will vary for each individual reader:

In Chapter One comfortably or uncomfortably, we started by 'thinking' outside of the box and looking at our own core values, beliefs and spirituality. You had the courage to talk about the Group Operations Director and what that means to you and if it meant nothing, what does?

In Chapter Two you looked at the strength within you and really put yourself under the microscope. You acknowledged where your stress lies, admitted if you were generally a positive person or a negative person, came clean as to whether you could drop your ego and be open and honest enough to walk in another's shoes.

In Chapter Three you educated yourself on different forms of exercise. Exercising your brain, foundations and choices as well as exercising nutritionally and physically. The biggest thing we looked at in Chapter Three was 'you' taking responsibility for 'you'.

In Chapter Four you moved into 'action' and figuring out how you were going to activate and implement all that you had learnt; intentions, goal setting and moving away from old patterns in order to create brand new ones. How cool is that!

In Chapter Five well, my goodness. You had the courage to look at 'love' and *is* the love you give and receive honest? You looked at the responsibility you must take for what you see in people and be honest about how you love different people. How proud of you am I!

In Chapter Six we looked at what a fantastic big '10' or '100%' you are, the five steps to taking action and again moving away from neglect in order to take *good* care of yourself.

In Chapter Seven you looked at what your life could be like and again worked on your goal setting and possible ideas to move into your 'real' life, the authentic you and realising who you are not!

In Chapter Eight you forgave. You began the process of cleaning up your own mess and started to work with forgiving yourself which is incredible –honestly, what more can I say?

So you see you have been practicing since chapter one. You have been taking little risks throughout this book by opening the many compartments of your life and exploring them. You have looked at and dealt with choice, forgiveness, love, options, fear and creating possibilities to name a few. If you think about it, you have been doing all of these things throughout your life; dealing with the relationship you have with your parents or losing a parent(s), family, peer pressure, school teachers, getting a job, losing a job, falling sick, bad relationships and even the experience you had of being born! The list goes on and these are just some of the things that have shaped and challenged you. What I hope is that you have been guided forward to this stage with a renewed creativity, confidence, optimism and realisation that the risks you previously did not take because you thought they were huge and a bit scary, are just not.

Finally, if you strip it right back and I am asking you now to take a look, it does not matter where you are, just take a good look around. Everything, every single solitary thing that you can see started with a 'thought'. If you are in a room and can see paint on walls, paint started as a thought, a light bulb started from just one thought. Flooring, clothes, make-up, cars, carpet, cutlery, cups, paper, bottles, tin foil, cling film, tennis balls, seating, storage containers, nail varnish, cuff links – the list is literally endless, so *we know* that thoughts become things. When you are thinking and feeling about what you do or do not want in life you are in a creative process and it will manifest into something. Therefore, if there is something in particular you would like to achieve that involves a bit of risk, do it now, make it a reality. Keep thinking and feeling positively about it and keep the inner negative voices out. Speak to yourself in a confident and encouraging way. If you have been reading this book and implementing all of the ideas then *you are* on the right track. Taking risks and even just living life in general takes time, patience, practice and persistence but most importantly daily practice.

People often say that motivation doesn't last. Well, neither does bathing that's why we recommend it daily.
Zig Ziglar

Now write down:

What have I found most beneficial about this chapter:

_____

_____

_____

_____

What do I need to do or in what way could I be thinking better in order to move forward:

_____

_____

_____

_____

Additional Notes:

CHAPTER TEN

KINDNESS, GRATITUDE & GRACE

Kindness is a language which the deaf can hear
and the blind can see.
Mark Twain

Be kinder to yourself and your needs. Understand and praise yourself fully for getting this far. So many people are afraid to look in the mirror and you have been looking both inside and out - all together now:

I AM BEAUTIFUL INSIDE & OUT

Jesse Jackson said you should never look down on anybody unless you're helping them up and he's right. It's equally important to be kind to others, it is *never* wasted. A kind word will cost you nothing but could completely change someone's day.

Today give a stranger one of your smiles. It might be the only
sunshine he sees all day.
P.S. I Love You compiled by H. Jackson Brown Jr.

*If you concentrate on finding whatever is good in every situation, you will discover that your life will suddenly be filled with **gratitude**, a feeling that nurtures the soul.*
Rabbi Harold Kushner

It would be beneficial for you to practice gratitude. For me personally, when I am deep in gratitude there is a feeling of joy, happiness and light in my body and mind. Even saying the word 'gratitude' or 'I feel gratitude for .....' just rolls off the tongue, it makes me smile.

When you say out loud what it is that you are grateful for, there is a feeling of 'opening' an expansion in your body. It is almost as if the whole body is replying back 'thank you! thank you for being grateful for all of the wondrous blessings in your life'.

When you express gratitude and you feel that lovely feeling in your body and good about yourself you are experiencing the *natural, organic* results of gratitude. If not then you may have conflicted feelings about what it is you are saying you are thankful for; the thing or person you picked, in which case you would need to address those conflicts first. Or, simply don't go down a list to be thankful for if you are not!

The Here & Now & What Am I Thankful For
Many years ago I went through quite a bit of personal trauma and I noticed in later years after the trauma was well and truly

over that I still struggled with staying in the 'here & now'. My past would pop into my head at the most awkward times and I would begin to worry about others and what they were going through to the detriment of my own health. I would mull over my future and '*was* I out the other end'. Was my breakdown going to come back and completely bite my backside off?

Then, one day driving to work a wee voice in my head kept saying 'look around you and stick to what you see. Look around you and stick to what you see'. It started off with me saying:

> I am in my car
> I feel my legs moving to change gear
> I feel my foot hit the accelerator and the break
> I see the clouds
> I feel the temperature in the car
> I like the interior in my car
> I hear my radio playing
> I am going to work
> I see the trees
> I see the traffic
> I see the lake. . .

Trust me, it went on and on, I could see loads. But it served its purpose and kept me in the 'here and now'. The more I did it the less I found myself mulling over the past, the future or even what I was going to be doing that weekend – it was great.

The list developed as I started to talk to myself, yes, talk to myself.

It was around 2010 coming into 2011 and things were really bad and I guess still are, for thousands of people. A friend of mine who is a top Quantity Surveyor was due her first child and had just been made redundant, and then her husband as well, it was awful. All over the place young professionals had top mark degrees, but no work in their chosen field. I found myself being incredibly grateful for all of the incredible blessings in *my* life.

Thank you for my lovely bed to sleep in and the duvet
that kept me warm last night
I am really glad I am going to work, there are so many
people being made redundant, God I am so lucky
I love that I have a wee car to get to work, thank you.
Thank you for my legs and that I can walk
Thank you for my feet to take me where I need to go
Thank you for my fingers
Thank you for my hair
Thank you for my nails
Thank you for my skin protecting my body
Oh my God, thank you for my beautiful heart
Thank you for my spine, pretty good for holding me up
Thank you for my toes
Thank you for my bladder

Thank you for my lungs

Thank you for my Parents

Thank you for my Nephew

Thank you for my Brothers & Sisters

Thank you for my family and friends

Thank you for every molecular structure that makes up my being

Thank you for insects

Thank you for the birds

Thank you for the ocean

Thank you for the clouds

Thank you for the trees

Thank you for colour

Thank you for my eyes that I can see the colours

Thank you for music

Thank you for my ears that I can hear the music

Thank you for my senses and faculties

Thank you for my talents and abilities

Thank you for my beautiful home to go home to

Thank you for the good times in my life

Thank you for the bad times, they have been incredible opportunities for me to grow….

Pretty much most days I am in my car on a minimum of a thirty minute drive and I can fill as much time allowed with all of the gifts I am humbly grateful for – **I <u>never</u> run out of things to be grateful and thankful for**.

If I were you I would make a start, *immediately*. I highly recommend this for several reasons:

1. It keeps you in the here & now:
I started doing this at a basic level, just looking around and saying out loud what I saw to keep me in the 'here & now' and it does! You don't have to only do this in the car when travelling, I use it whenever I feel I need to. If I am at home with too much time on my hands and my head starts to get chatty with old negative voices I'll use this exercise. If I feel I'm getting overwhelmed, I use it and so on.

2. It makes you fully aware & changes the experience of the 'life' you are having:
In looking around at what I saw I was very effectively utilising 'applied awareness'. I could write another book on this and anyone who has been to my workshops will know about applied awareness. There is a massive difference between being aware and applying awareness. When I was actively looking and saying out loud what I was seeing, my journey to work completely changed. I had no idea how much beauty, colour and <u>life</u> I see on every single journey, it was fantastic and I loved it!

3. It promotes & reinforces an incredibly healthy attitude:
Many years ago a colleague approached me in work and said

'can I ask you something'. I said 'yes, no bother'. She continued on to say 'I've never seen you in bad form. You are always so enthusiastic, really buzzing. I love being on shift when you are here'. Of course I responded. 'Well, thank you very much for the compliment but do you really think I don't get disappointed, or angry? I do, it's just that it does not serve me. I'll probably be disappointed for 15-20 minutes but then I'll move on, I will shift my thinking to something better because it's not doing me any favours'. She started laughing and said 'I need to practice a bit of that'. We all do!

I have said in previous chapters when you do one thing, you non-consciously start doing others without realising at all. I really do feel (for me!) that another benefit of being thankful for my blessings and saying each out loud and what I see through my eyes, fills me with so much gratitude for life and all of the wonderful people and experiences in my life that the low level stuff or negatives that can get you down from time to time, just get lost in it. **They lose their power** and they **lose their power over me.**

Being thankful and showing gratitude has made a profound difference in my life. But remember how this chapter opened. It's not just saying 'thank you' although even if you started with that it will equally have a profound effect. You need to practice until naturally you show:

GRATITUDE (grat·i·tude); The quality of being thankful; readiness to show appreciation for and to <u>return kindness.</u>

Gratitude unlocks the fullness of life. It turns what we have into enough, and more. It turns denial into acceptance, chaos into order, confusion into clarity... It turns problems into gifts, failures into success, the unexpected into perfect timing, and mistakes into important events. Gratitude makes sense of our past, brings peace for today and creates a vision for tomorrow.
Melodie Beattie

Practice being grateful every day. If you don't know where to start or how, then say my list every day until you think of your own, there are bound to be similarities in there. At the end of the day, if you are not grateful for what you already do have in your life what on earth makes you think you will blessed with more?

GRACE

*Infuse your life with action. Don't wait for it to happen. Make it happen. Make your own future. Make your own hope. Make your own love. And whatever your beliefs, honor your creator, not by passively waiting for grace to come down from upon high, but by doing what you can to make **grace** happen... yourself, right now, right down here on Earth.*
Bradley Whitford

Grace is something that is usually associated with spirituality or God. However, it is not the entirety of revealed truth or the sacraments I wish to address but the grace we have been blessed with, your own 'in-built' grace and doing what you can to make grace happen. Even if you do not have a God or believe in prayer you must agree with 'good', otherwise you are reading the wrong book for it is *all* about what is good in life and most importantly what is **good in you**.

You have been reading this and looking at yourself, your life and I am sure there have been ups and downs. Times when you did one of the exercises, understood it and got a lot from it. Then others where you thought 'What on earth is Sinéad asking me to do here?' not to mention the general ongoing day to day stresses and strains of life. You have continued with determination and courage, so when I talk about in built grace I mean to keep going, keep being courageous, making things happen and make your own grace.

Courage is grace under pressure.
Ernest Hemingway

Now write down:

What have I found most beneficial about this chapter:

_____

_____

_____

_____

What do I need to do or in what way could I be thinking better in order to move forward:

_____

_____

_____

_____

Additional Notes:

166

CHAPTER 11

THE GRAND FINALE

A smooth sea never made a skilled sailor
Author Unknown

My existence has been wonderful, with all of its ups and downs I have still achieved so much and it is as a result of some of the strategies and approaches I have shared in this book.

This book is repetitive. I have asked you constantly to look at yourself, how you think and how you feel. Self expression is such a crucial necessity of human nature and as you have worked through this book filling in all of the blanks and expressing yourself; desires, morals, values and your opinions, it has now become a personal life-coach journal that *you* have created. I ask that you please take the opportunity from time to time, to reflect over it and the details you have completed in chapters and your personal thoughts on the 'note's' pages. It is a great way to see clearly all that you have achieved.

Have you ever read or heard a riddle that is impossible to work out but when you are given the answer it is so clear, simple and easy? When you make a start on living you begin to realise how easy it actually is. You already have the answers, the knowledge and the power within you. All you have to do is put it into practice and put your wonderful talents, abilities, knowledge and mind to great use. Everyone can do something to bring themselves a little closer or a lot closer to their hopes and dreams. As I said in chapter three when you were learning about operating that Master Key; take your foot off the brake and put it on the accelerator. Stop looking behind you so that you can see all of the wonderful possibilities that lie ahead of you. The following is my final top ten tips, small things you can do that will have a big impact on your existence.

1. Show a genuine interest in others, it is great for your own self development.

2. Smile, people just look so much better when they smile.

3. Create good will *not* bad, it can literally lift your soul when you provide a random act of kindness.

4. Remember that envy is nothing more than your own ignorance or lack of belief in your own gifts. Believe in yourself and believe in your gifts.

5. Appreciate what you have and give thanks to avoid the guilt.

6. Make yourself accountable, when you take responsibility you will feel virtuous which is great for the body, mind and soul.

7. Practice the art of visualisation it, is well documented how powerful this is. Visualise your dreams actually happening, what you would feel like to the point of seeing what you are wearing! Every detail.

8. The number one cause of illness and disease is an unhealthy lifestyle and an unhealthy response to stress. Keep practicing the techniques in this book so that they become a habit, improve your lifestyle and help keep your response to stress healthy and ailments at bay or away!

9. Attitude will always be the major factor in the success of any recovery, do not have an attitude that stinks.

10. Be kind even to strangers on the street. Absolutely everyone is up against something and remember a smile costs you nothing.

I would be absolutely thrilled if in just reading this book it has helped improve your life - that was the plan! However, these words will only help you understand. It is only through applying the information and actual 'experience' that will allow you to *know*. Do this book justice. Go out there and experience it, the sheer joy of living! Become the skilled sailor of your life.

Minister & The Soap Maker

A minister and a soap maker went for a walk together. The soap maker said, "What good is religion? Look at all the trouble and misery of the world which still remains, even after thousands of years of preaching about goodness and truth and peace. If religion is so good and true why did all these prayers and sermons not make a difference?"

The minister said nothing. They continued walking until he noticed a child playing in the gutter. Then the minister said, "Look at that child. You say that soap makes people clean, but see the dirt on that youngster. Of what good is soap? With all the soap in the world, over all these years, the child is still filthy. I wonder how effective soap is, after all!"

The soap maker protested. "But, soap cannot do any good unless it is applied!"

"Exactly!" replied the minister.

Author Unknown

Now write down:

What have I found most beneficial about this book and why is it so brilliant! (LOL!!!):

_____

_____

_____

_____

What do I need to do or in what way could I be thinking better in order to move forward:

_____

_____

_____

_____

Additional Notes:

A Final Message From Sinead

Life is like a piano, the white keys represent happiness and black keys represent sadness. But as you go through life's journey, remember that the black keys also create music.
Author Unknown

We have arrived at the end of our book and I cannot thank you enough for spending this time with me. I started this book in January 2003. Little did I realise that it would take over 10 years to complete, my goodness what a journey.

Timing can sometimes be everything. For some reading this book it may be like watching a movie. I have watched movies and got nothing from them and then saw the same movie a couple of years down the line and thought it was fantastic. For some, this book may have landed in your lap at the perfect time and for others it may be reinforcing everything you already knew anyway. A gentle reminder can often be a good thing and I hope it has been for you.

Please remember that this is not about creating a business empire or flying to the moon. It is about your life and what you would like to do with it, how *you* would like your life to be. There is not one person who cannot improve the quality of their life by changing their thoughts about themselves or their circumstances. The information in this book is not airy fairy but is supported by science; you *can* rewire the patterns in the brain and create new neural pathways all the time.

I called this book 'She's Got The Whole World' because I do. I have a massive contribution to make to the world and this book is just one aspect of it. My friend, life is not perfect. It can be graceful, happy, strong-minded, hard-wearing and tragic all in one. I believe in the beauty of life, the beauty of love and all that it holds. So when your life seems imperfect or defective in some way maybe it's just how you are looking at it, remember that every negative has a plus. I told you at the start of this book that I wanted to help you feel good about yourself again and I hope that you do. You too have a massive contribution to make in this world, take action and give yourself a life worth living. I *have* got the whole world in my hands and so do you.

Thank you for reading, sending you much love.
Sinéad McGarrigle

She's Got The Whole World